MEDIEVAL VIEWS OF THE COSMOS

MEDIEVAL VIEWS OF THE COSMOS

by

E. Edson and E. Savage-Smith

BODLEIAN LIBRARY · UNIVERSITY OF OXFORD

First published in 2004 by The Bodleian Library
Broad Street
Oxford OX1 3BG

ISBN 1 85124 184 1

Designed by Dot Little
Diagram artwork by Tyra Till and John Shiel

Printed and bound by the University Press, Cambridge

British Library Catalogue in Publishing Data
A CIP record of this publication is available from the British Library

Cover: in relief: the Earth in relation to the four elements (earth, air, fire, water), the winds,
and the seasons (as represented by the 12 zodiacal signs. MS. Arab. c. 90, fol. 21b (12th-13th
century). Planispheric astrolabe made in 1081-2 (474 H) in the Spanish city of Guadalajara by
Muḥammad ibn Saʿīd al-Ṣabbān, known as Ibn Mashshāṭ al-Saraqusṭī al-Aṣṭurlābī ('the
astrolabe-maker of Saragossa'). Oxford, Museum of the History of Science, Inv. no. 52473.

Frontispiece: God the Creator seated, circumscribing the globe with compasses, from the *Bible
moralisée*, MS. Bodl. 270b, fol. 1v (Paris, *c.*1235-45).

Back cover: God creating the sun, moon and stars from the creation cycle in the Ashmole
Bestiary. MS. Ashmole 1511, fol. 5v (English, early 13th century).

Contents

Christian and Islamic Dates

The Muslim calendar is a lunar one of 354 days beginning from the day of the Emigration (Hijrah) of the Prophet Muḥammad from Mecca to Medina, which occurred on the 16th of July 622 of the Christian calendar. Consequently, Muslim dates to not correspond directly to those of the Christian era (AD) commonly used today in Europe and the US. For convenience, most dates in this book will be those of the Christian calendar. General references to a century rather than a specific year refer to centuries of the Christian era. For example, ninth century refers to the years 800–899 AD (which in the Muslim calendar would be 184–287). The designation AD will be used only when there is need to distinguish a date from an earlier BC date. The Muslim calendar is designated by H.

Manuscript Format and References

The contents of medieval manuscripts are not usually numbered by pages but rather by folios (or leaves) each of which has two sides. In Western manuscripts, written in languages reading from left to right, the two sides of a folio are designated either r (*recto*) or v (*verso*). In manuscripts written in languages reading from right to left, such as Arabic, Hebrew, and Persian, the sides of a folio are referred to in the sequence read as 'a' and 'b'.

Foreword

To my embarrassment I have to confess that for many years my interest in medieval maps was confined to the use of a copy of the fourteenth-century Gough Map as decoration for a coffee-table I'd bought. But then in 2002, the BBC producer Mark Rickards invited me to make a four-part series for Radio 4 under the title *The Medieval Ball*. Having always thought that maps were rather visual things the proposal to make a programme for radio on the subject struck me as a curious one. The idea of doing four such programmes and confining them to medieval maps struck me as so down-right ludicrous that I couldn't say no.

Thus it was that I found myself drawn into this fascinating subject, and I had the opportunity of meeting many of the leading authorities in the field such as Emilie Savage-Smith, Peter Barber and Evelyn Edson. And of course, I soon discovered that there is much more to medieval maps than meets the eye.

The thing that appeals most to me about the study of medieval maps is that it explodes many of our common prejudices about the people of the Middle Ages. For example, it is currently fashionable to think of our medieval forebears as ignorant and simple-minded. The maps which they left behind seem to reinforce this reputation. After all who could take seriously a map of the world that shows the location of the Garden of Eden, the Tower of Babel, Noah's Ark and Jason's Golden Fleece? And yet, in mocking the simplicity of our ancestors it is often we who are betraying our own ignorance. As Evelyn Edson and Emilie Savage-Smith demonstrate in this book, the *mappae mundi* of the thirteenth and fourteenth centuries were not intended as geographical charts of the physical world. They were rather 'attempts to explore theological and historical aspects of space' (see p. 118).

In the same way, most people today seem to be convinced that the folk of the Middle Ages believed the world was flat, when it is clear that they didn't. Plato's cosmology, 'which was so important in the medieval view of the cosmos' (see p. 22) had the spherical earth at its centre. The thirteenth-century friar and 'philosopher', Roger Bacon, wrote that the curvature of the earth explains why we can see further from higher elevations.

So why do we believe that medieval people thought the world was flat? The chief culprit was an American journalist by the name of Washington Irving, who in 1828 published a biography of Christopher Columbus. In this illuminating tome he described his hero confronting the Church fathers at Salamanca, where they accused him of heresy for saying the world was round, when the Church taught that it was flat. It was a dramatic scene and became the subject of many paintings. The only trouble is that Washington Irving made it up. There was no confrontation such as he describes, and the Church certainly never taught that the world was flat. Indeed, Nicholas Oresme, the Bishop of Lisieux and councillor of Charles V, begins one of his books by saying: The world is round like a ball.

It's all baloney, and yet it fits so neatly into our modern assumption that we are so much cleverer and more intelligent than people in the past, that it seems impossible to eradicate the misconception.
This is why I think the study of the medieval view of the cosmos can contribute a lot to our reassessment of our medieval predecessors. Perhaps, even more importantly, this book, makes plain the common heritage of Christian and Islamic scientific knowledge in medieval times. It also brings out the vital intercourse between the Christian and Islamic worlds, prior to the Crusades, and thereby sets a vital context against which we can view many of the current conflicts in the modern world.

Medieval Views of the Cosmos offers the reader a chance to reassess the past, and a yardstick against which to measure the future.

Terry Jones

Introduction: The Medieval Cosmos

Once upon a time the universe had meaning. In place of our modern idea of formless, endless space, scattered sparsely and randomly with stars, planets, asteroids, black holes, pulsars, and quasars, there was a tightly structured, hierarchical system centred around the earth and the human race. At every level was found a moral lesson for humanity and a satisfying metaphor for the nature of God (frontispiece and back cover). All had its beginning in the divine command, 'Let there be light!', instead of the undignified Big Bang. Not only was this system morally and spiritually meaningful, it was reinforced by simple observation and common sense.

In order to understand the medieval world view, C.S. Lewis suggests that you:

> …go out on a starry night and walk about for half an hour trying to see the sky in terms of the old cosmology. Remember that you now have an absolute Up and Down. The Earth is really the centre, really the lowest place; movement to it from whatever direction is downward movement. As a modern, you located the stars at a very great distance. For distance you must now substitute that very special, and far less abstract, sort of distance which we call height; height, which speaks immediately to our muscles and nerves. The Medieval Model is vertiginous. And the fact that the height of the stars in the medieval astronomy is very small compared with their distance in the modern, will turn out not to have the kind of importance you anticipated. For thought and imagination, ten million miles and a thousand million are much the same. Both can be conceived (that is, we can do sums with both) and neither can be imagined; and the more imagination we have the better we shall know this. The really important difference is that the medieval universe, while unimaginably

large, was also unambiguously finite. And one unexpected result of this is to make the smallness of Earth more vividly felt. In our universe she is small, no doubt; but so are the galaxies, so is everything—and so what? But in theirs there was an absolute standard of comparison. The furthest sphere, Dante's *maggior corpo* is, quite simply, the largest object in existence. The word 'small' as applied to Earth thus takes on a far more absolute significance. Again, because the medieval universe is finite, it has a shape, the perfect spherical shape, containing within itself an ordered variety. Hence to look out on the night sky with modern eyes is like looking out over a sea that fades away into mist, or looking about one in a trackless forest—trees forever and no horizon. To look up at the towering medieval universe is much more like looking at a great building. The 'space' of modern astronomy may arouse terror, or bewilderment or vague reverie; the spheres of the old present us with an object in which the mind can rest, overwhelming in its greatness but satisfying in its harmony.[1]

The earth was the centre of this system of concentric transparent spheres; it was also the lowest point and the scene of change, birth, death, and decay and therefore of sorrow and loss. As one ascended to

Figure 1. Spheres of the heavens, from John of Sacrobosco, *De sphaera* (early 13th cent.), with earth at the centre and the Prime Mover at the outer edge. MS. Ashmole 1522, fol. 25r (English, mid-14th century).

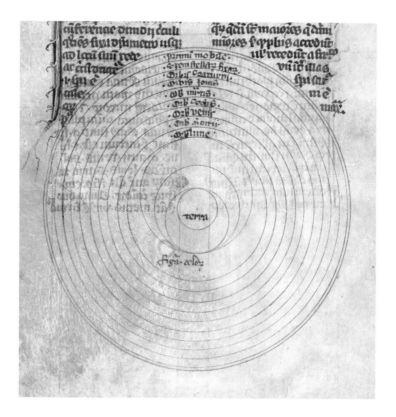

each of the spheres which surrounded the earth, one advanced toward greater light, the symbol of spirituality. Above, beyond the sphere of the moon, there was no change, no death. All was suffused with light and joy. This classical scheme shaped both Islamic and Christian thinking in the Middle Ages (Figure 1).

Dante's fourteenth-century poetic and philosophical description of this system in the *Divine Comedy* is one of the most complete and eloquent, though he bases his ideas on clearly established precedents. The planets are not mere chunks of matter but 'Intelligences' and to each a quality is assigned, loosely related to the pagan god for which it was named: in Mercury, honour; in Venus, love; in Mars, noble war; in Jupiter, just government; in Saturn, contemplation. The Sun, between Venus and Mars, being the maximum of light the human eye can behold, is dedicated by Dante to the contemplation of the Trinity, and this sphere is inhabited by the doctors of the Church. Beyond the planets one approaches the sphere of the stars, where the Apostles are found. At this point Beatrice, Dante's angelic guide, tells him to look back: 'See how vast a universe I have put beneath your feet, bright sphere on bright sphere.' And Dante, looking down, says, 'My eyes went back through the seven spheres below, and I saw this globe, so small, so lost in space, I had to smile at such a sorry show.' He ascends beyond the stars to the outer sphere of the angels, the Empyrean or Primum Mobile. Here the light is so intense that the poet is temporarily blinded with his vision of the divine, for the outermost sphere is suffused with the presence of God. Dante says, 'I saw a Point that radiated light of such intensity that the eye it strikes must close or ever after lose its sight.' [2]

Our universe is perhaps more egalitarian, but the medieval world admired hierarchy both on earth and in the heavens. Shakespeare, writing in the late sixteenth century, gives us a paean to class structure in *Troilus and Cressida*, in a speech assigned to Ulysses:

> The heavens themselves, the planets, and this centre
> Observe degree, priority, and place,
> Insisture, course, proportion, season, form,
> Office, and custom, in all line of order;
> . . . But when the planets
> In evil mixture to disorder wander,
> What plagues and what portents, what mutiny,
> What raging of the sea, shaking of earth,

Commotion in the winds! Frights, changes, horrors
Divert and crack, rend and deracinate
The unity and married calm of states
Quite from their fixure! O, when degree is shak'd,
Which is the ladder to all high designs,
Then enterprise is sick! How could communities,
Degrees in schools and brotherhoods in cities,
Peaceful commerce from dividable shores,
The primogenity and due of birth,
Prerogative of age, crowns, scepters, laurels,
But, by degree, stand in authentic place?
Take but degree away, untune that string,
And hark what discord follows! [3]

Each of the planets, mounted on a transparent sphere which allowed the light to shine through, moved unceasingly in its proper orbit as established and set in motion by God. The intervals between the spheres were in the same proportion as the musical intervals discovered by Pythagoras in the sixth century BC, and thus, as the spheres revolved, they made harmonious music (see Figure 2). This world of radiance, music, and intelligence—how different from the universe we now imagine!

Beyond the moon the laws of earthly physics did not exist. Motion was perfect, spherical motion, whereas on earth motion was either natural, in a straight line, falling toward the centre, impelled by gravity, or violent, such as an arrow shot from a bow. Unlike objects on earth, the heavens were not made of earthly elements but of some heavenly substance impervious to change—Aristotle called it aether, the fifth element or quintessence. The heavenly bodies were weightless, and since God had set them in motion, they would continue to revolve in their eternal, perfect orbits, never deviating or falling.

The elements in the sublunar sphere were four—fire, air, water, and earth, in descending order with the heaviest element on the bottom (see Figure 3). These elements were also imagined as spheres surrounding the earth, with the outermost sphere of fire being that of the moon. Each element was composed of two of the four basic qualities, which were hot, cold, wet, and dry; that is, earth was cold and dry, water cold and wet, air hot and wet, and fire hot and dry. These elemental combinations led, in the medieval mind, to numerous correspondences—another characteristic of the universe, that all is

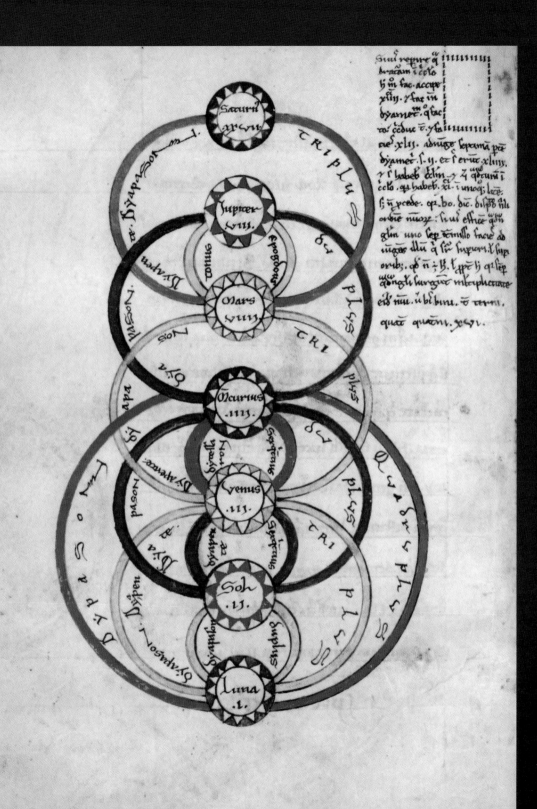

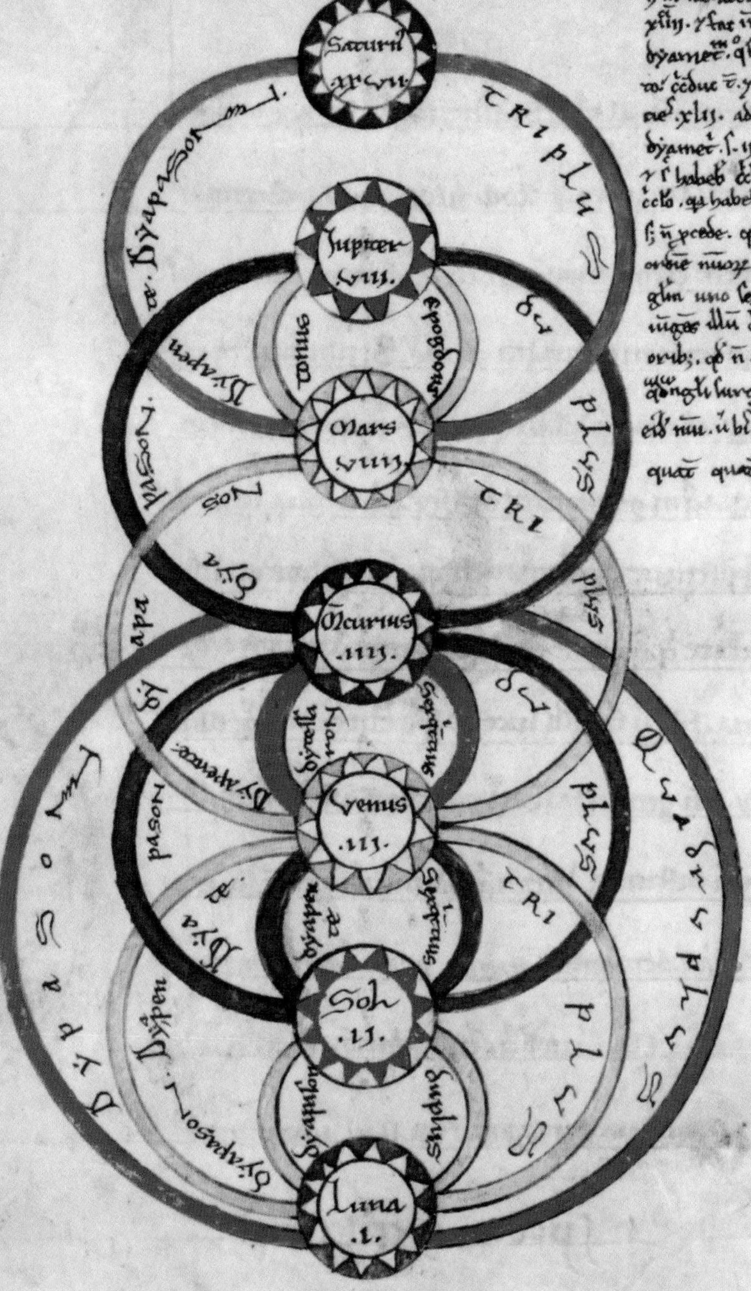
Saturn
Jupiter
Mars
Mercurius
.iiii.
Venus
.iii.
Soli
.ii.
Luna
.i.
Triplus
Quadruplus
Tonus
Epogdous
Duplus

Sicut reperire q[ua]d[r]atum i[n] celo
h[oc] m[odo] fac. accipe
xliii. [et] fac in
dyamet[ro] q[uadrata]c
ta c[on]cedit[ur] [et] sta

re[n]s. xlii. adiunge separata[m] per
dyametr[um] s[cilicet] .ii. et s[ic] erit. xliiii.
[et] s[ic] habeb[is] cclm [et] q[ua]drantu[m] i[n]
celo. q[ua]s habeb[is]. xi. i[n] unoq[uo]q[ue] late[re].
s[ed] n[on] p[ro]cede. q[uia]. bo. dic. disp[ositi]o nil
orbis num[er]or[um]: sicut effic[it] q[ua]dran
glu[m] uno sep[t]e[m] t[er]minis facie[n]s ad
iugas illu[m] q[uo]d s[it] superiori. t[er] supi
orib[us]; q[uo]d n[on] e[st]. h[oc] t[ame]n ap[er]te h[oc] q[uia] sep
q[ua]dra[n]guli surgu[n]t multiplicat[ur]
eis nu[mer]i. u[bi] b[is] bini. [et] t[er] t[er]ni.
quat[er] quat[er]ni. xxvi.

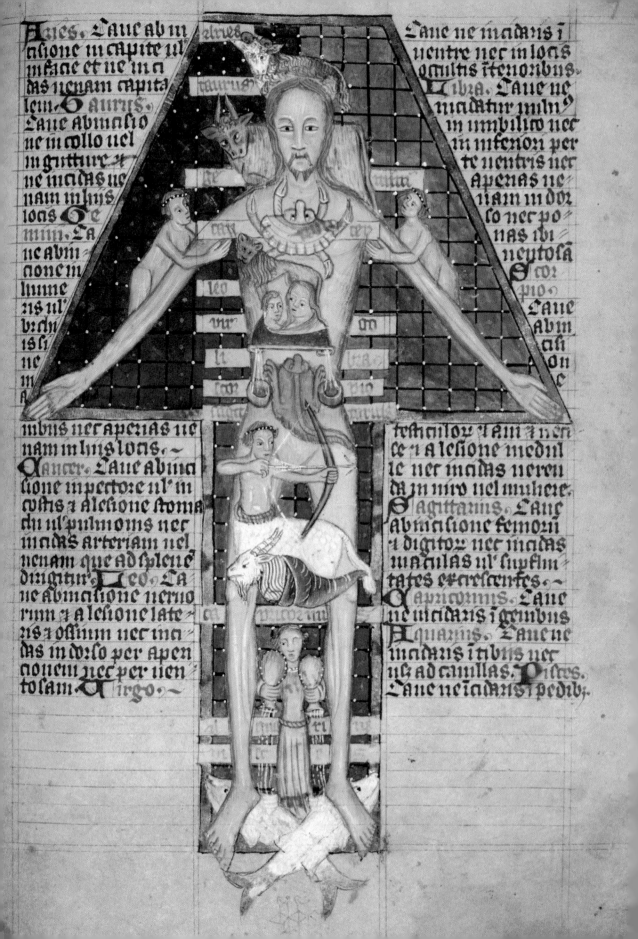

Aries. Caue ab in
cisione in capite ul'
in facie et ne in ci
das uenam capita
lem. Taurus.
Caue ab incisio
ne in collo uel
in gutture et
ne incidas ue
nam in huius
locis. Ge
mini. Ca
ue ab in
cisione in
lune
ns ul'
brach
is si
ne
in
...

...mbus nec aperias ue
nam in huius locis.
Cancer. Caue ab inci
sione in pectore ul' in
costis et a lesione stoma
chi ul' pulmonis nec
incidas arteriam uel
uenam que ad splene
dirigitur. Leo. Ca
ue ab incisione neruo
rum et a lesione late
ris et ossium nec inci
das in dorso per apen
cionem nec per uen
tosam. Virgo.

Caue ne incidas in
uentre nec in locis
occultis interioribus.
Libra. Caue ne
incidatur mulier
in umbilico nec
in inferiori per
te uentris nec
aperias ue
nam in dor
so nec po
nas ibi
uentosam.
Scor
pio.
Caue
ab in
cisi
on

testiculorum et ani et ner
ce et a lesione medul
le nec incidas uerē
da in uiro uel muliere.
Sagittarius. Caue
ab incisione femorū
et digitorū nec incidas
maculas ul' superflui
tates excrescentes.
Capricornus. Caue
ne incidas in genibus.
Aquarius. Caue ne
incidas in tibiis nec
uenis ad cauillas. Pisces.
Caue ne incidas in pedibus.

connected. The human body was thought of as a microcosm, reflecting the larger universe, or macrocosm, and also containing the four elements (see Figure 4). The qualities were related to the humours, fluids in the human body, which in turn were related to one's basic personality or outlook on life as well as one's health. The different humours corresponded to the different seasons, and in turn to the ages of man or stages of life. Man was also influenced by the soil on which he was born, each territory being under the influence of a particular planet (though there was not complete agreement on which planet governed which place) and he was governed by the time of his birth, including the dominant planet and zodiac sign. It is no wonder that astrology was a popular and highly regarded science throughout the Middle Ages in both the Islamic and Christian worlds. Even though Christian theology was based firmly on free will, it was clear that one's temperament and 'stars' had a great influence on one's fate. In the Islamic world, even though some considered astrology to contradict the strict omnipotence of God and to offer dangerous competition to religion, it nonetheless provided for many an explanation of man's role within the structure of the universe (see Figure 5).

The form of the earth below had surprisingly few constraints imposed by theology, in either Christianity or Islam. The Bible is somewhat vague on the cosmos, outside the sweeping words of Genesis 1. Medieval geographers were left to ponder the meaning of such phrases as 'the waters above the earth and the waters under the earth' (see Figure 6) or Job's remark about the earth being suspended on nothing (Job 26:7), and by the revelation in the apocryphal Esdras that only one-seventh of the earth's surface was covered by water (2 Esdras 6:42). The four corners of the earth (Rev. 7:1) was another expression that few took literally. Similarly, the Qur'ān says of the earth only that it is spread wide like a carpet and held firmly in place by mountains (for example 13:3 and 15:19) and that it is one of seven earths, corresponding to the seven heavens (65:12). Yet the other earths were not specified and literalist interpretations not encouraged.

In fact, the Middle Ages took what they understood of Greek cosmology—transmitted to Europe by Roman and early Christian popularizers and to the Middle East by ninth-century translators in Baghdad—and made it their own. One such idea was the spherical form of the earth.

Figure 4 *left*. Signs of the zodiac superimposed on the human body to indicate that blood-letting from that part is unadvisable when the moon is in that sign. MS. Ashmole 391, item 5, fol. 9r (late 14th century).

Figure 5. The Earth in relation to the
four elements (earth, air, fire, water),
the winds, and the seasons (as
represented by the 12 zodiacal signs),
MS. Arab. c. 90, fol. 21b (12th-13th
century).

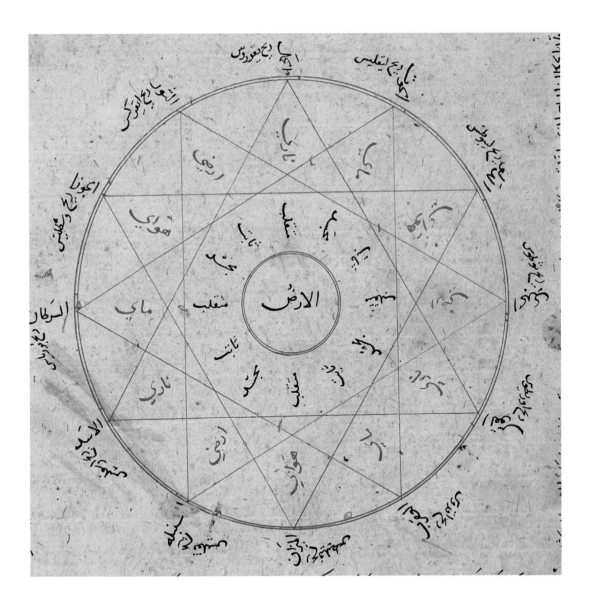

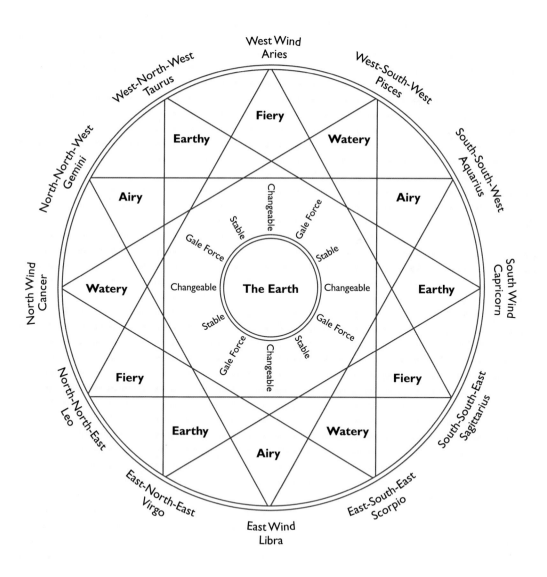

The motions of the cosmos had a profound impact on the timing of religious rituals in both Christianity and Islam. The Muslim calendar is a strictly lunar one, with the start of the fasting month of Ramadān (and other months) determined by the first sighting of the new moon. The times for the five obligatory daily prayers are determined by sunrise and sunset. Thus timekeeping and knowledge of astronomical matters are essential to a muezzin calling from a minaret the hours of prayer, which differ from one day to the next and from one locale to another. Moreover, not only time but geography and geometry are essential elements in Islamic religious observance because of the obligation to pray and perform various ritual acts while facing towards the sacred shrine of the Ka'ba in Mecca. This requirement gave rise to tables, maps, and instruments to assist in solving the difficult problem of determining angular distances between two localities on a spherical earth (see Figure 7). The centrality of astronomy and mathematics to everyday religious life was a major reason why these disciplines thrived in the medieval Islamic world.

Figure 6 *left.* God creating the firmament to divide the waters from the waters, from the creation cycle in the Ashmole Bestiary. MS. Ashmole 1511, fol. 4v. (English, early 13th century).

Figure 7 *below.* A Qibla diagram of 1196 from a treatise by the Egyptian scholar al-Dimyāṭī, showing the directions to be faced toward Mecca from four different localities (Aleppo, Damascus, Jerusalem and Cairo). MS. Marsh 592, fol. 88b.

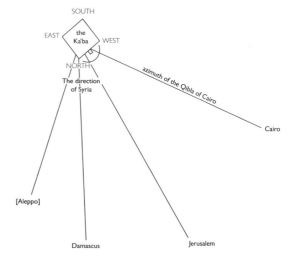

Figure 8. Calendar showing the age of the moon on the calends (first day) of each month, in order to coordinate the lunar and solar cycles over a period of 19 years. Oxford, St John's College, MS. 17, fol. 27r (English, 1110).

For Christians the celebration of Easter and its attendant moveable feasts also required a rather sophisticated understanding of heavenly motion. Easter was decreed by the Church to be on the first Sunday after the first full moon following the spring equinox. This date was carefully chosen because it was the day of maximum light—twelve hours of daylight followed by twelve hours of full moonlight. Determining the exact date of Easter required the coordination of three calendars—the solar, the lunar, and the seven-day week. The science of setting the proper date for Easter was called the computus and its calculations appear in many astronomical manuscripts, keeping astronomy alive during some of the darker days of the European medieval era. The establishment of the most important festival in the Christian year put cosmic and human time in harmony and is symbolic of the way the entire system functioned in the Middle Ages (see Figure 8).

On the Greek foundation, medieval scholars on both sides of the Mediterranean constructed a cosmological model that was completely satisfying on every level, so much so that its overthrow in the seventeenth century caused a profound spiritual and psychological disorientation from which we have yet to recover.

Hec rota pxi & viii. cycli decennouennalis annos p que epacte curr̄. indicat q̄ta sit luna p̄sin-
gl̄os annos. in kl̄das singl̄orum mensium. Sumpto initio abeo loco ubi menses sunt ad-
scripti. habentes iuxta se notatas lunas kalend̄arum singl̄orum mensium primi anni
prefati cycli. & sic deinceps p̄ singl̄as linearū + mensium kl̄.

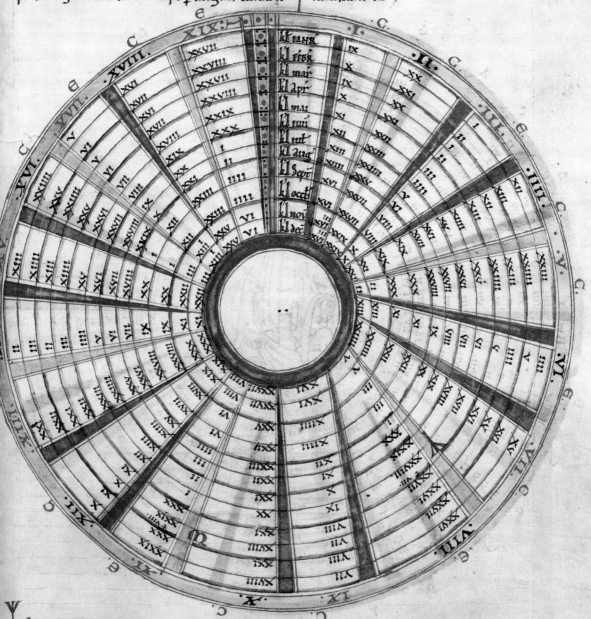

Sec̄m hoc argumentum. viij anno. x v iij. in kalendas mai luna ponitur
x x v iij. sed propter embolismum martii mensis. x x v i j. p̄batur existere.
Anno uero x j. cycli x v iiij li. iuxta hoc argumentum luna martii mensis
apponitur x x ix. cum x x v iij. existere doceatur

I

Greek and Roman Heritage

The accomplishments of the ancient Greeks in cosmology began with
the free-wheeling speculations of philosophers in the sixth century BC
living in Ionia, on the west coast of Asia Minor. Instead of a universe
directed by the whims and jealousies of an unruly collection of anthro-
pomorphic gods, the Ionians sought a variety of rationalistic explanations for cosmic events and began to construct an image of the universe as a whole. Was there only one world, or were there multiple
worlds? Was there a single element basic to all creation, and if so, what
was it? In the opinion of Heraclitus (d. 480 BC), this element was fire;
to Thales (d. c.547 BC), water. For 1500 years the Babylonians had been
assiduously collecting astronomical observations, but the early Greek
philosophers seem to have been too imaginative to be limited by such
pedantry. It was not until a century later that observation and theoriz-
ing were joined in a fruitful partnership. The cosmology of Plato
(c.429–347 BC), so important to the medieval view of the cosmos,
merged science and philosophy to form a true system. Principally set
forth in his dialogue the *Timaeus*, Plato's universe had the spherical
earth at its centre, surrounded by the great sphere of the heavens. Plato
believed that the universe was not eternal but had been created by an
intelligent and beneficent creator, who found the four elements of
matter in chaos and shaped them into a system. This was vital for
Christians and Muslims, who were eventually to inherit this system.
The creator was guided by principles such as the appreciation of beauty
and order. For example, the universe took a spherical shape because
the sphere was the most perfect and aesthetically pleasing of all forms.
Whereas the ancient gods had interfered with nature at their pleas-
ure—raising storms, producing monstrous births, eclipsing the sun—
Plato believed that the creator had made the laws of nature and,
because of his love for them and their essential rightness, would never
violate them, though he might have the power to do so. Thus a

mighty blow was dealt to omens and portents, as well as the practice of trying to appease the gods by offering up material sacrifices.

Building on the work of astronomers, such as his younger contemporary Eudoxus of Cnidus, Plato accounted for the errant motion of the planets by hypothesizing a series of individual circular movements for them, in addition to the major revolving sphere. These spheres, centred on the earth, had to be multiple in order to explain the complexity of planetary motion, and the result was a great nest of cosmic spheres all revolving around the stationary earth (see Figure 9).

Figure 9. Earth at the centre enclosed by the spheres of the Moon, Mercury, Venus, the Sun, Mars, Jupiter, Saturn, and the stars (3 bands: the 12 Zodiacal Houses, major stars, and the 28 'lunar mansions'), from an autograph copy made in 1333 of an Arabic treatise on timekeeping. MS. Bodl. Or. 133, fols. 117b–118a (Egypt, 1333).

Figure 10. In his dream Scipio is
shown the Seven Spheres and the
Milky Way by his father and
grandfather, from Cicero's *Dream of
Scipio* with Macrobius' Commentary.
MS. Canon. Class. Lat. 257, fol. 1v.
(Bologna, 1383).

The magnificent work of Aristotle (d. 322 BC) built on that of Plato.
Ptolemy, who lived in Alexandria from about 90 to 168 AD, carried
the tradition of Greek science into a period when the political power
of Greece had vanished, though her intellectual capacities were as acute
as ever. Virtually all the Greek scientific writings and most of Aristotle's books were translated into Arabic in the ninth century and were
widely available thereafter in the Arabic-speaking areas of the medieval
world. However, almost none of this work survived in Europe and it
had to be reintroduced in the twelfth century from the Islamic world.
The body of Greek scientific thought passing to the European West in
the early Middle Ages travelled through the narrow pipeline of Roman
encyclopaedists, commentators, and popularizers. Although the
Romans had had full access to Greek philosophy and many members
of the upper classes were bilingual, they tended to regard science as a
leisure-time pursuit and had little interest in adding to any branch of
knowledge lacking practical uses. In the first century BC, Cicero
translated into Latin Plato's *Timaeus* and the astronomical poem by
Aratus written about 250 BC. Nevertheless, most Greek scientific works
remained in Greek and were probably little read.

The early medieval European view of the universe was basically
Platonic, not only because Plato's ideas were most in harmony with
Christianity, but also because the texts that survived the general
holocaust of intellectual life in the sixth and seventh centuries of our
era were largely those of neo-Platonist authors, such as Augustine
(354–430), Macrobius (about 400 AD), and Martianus Capella (writing
about 410–429). The anti-intellectualism of some of the early Christians, such as Tertullian and Lactantius, was tempered by Augustine,
who suggested that they follow the model of the Hebrews in 'despoil-
ing the Egyptians' before fleeing to the Promised Land (Exodus 12:36).
Among the spoils of classical civilisation were the works of natural
philosophy. The late-antique encyclopaedists tried to save something
from the classical inheritance and were successful in passing on a digest
of astronomical lore, not all of which was clearly understood even by
them, much less by their hopeful medieval readers. Regrettably,
projects by Boethius (*c.*480–524) and Cassiodorus (*c.*487–583) to
assemble libraries and commentaries on all of classical knowledge were
never completed. Before the twelfth century, then, the scientific
heritage of the Greeks lived on in the West through a small number of
works, such as Chalcidius's commentary on the *Timaeus*, written in the
fourth century, and Macrobius's exposition of the *Dream of Scipio*
recounted in Cicero's *De re publica* (Figure 10).

Figure 11. Diagram attributed to the tenth-century English monk Byrhtferth: a symphony of correspondences including cardinal directions, winds, elements, qualities, ages of man, seasons, months, signs of the zodiac. Oxford, St John's College, MS. 17, fol. 7v (English, 1110).

Isidore of Seville (c.560–636) and Bede of Northumberland (673–735), the most important western scientific thinkers of the early medieval period, both wrote brief, popular treatises on natural phenomena entitled *De natura rerum*. Both were churchmen, as all educated men in the West now were, and their interests were not in science for its own sake but as it illuminated the Christian faith and related to practical endeavours. Thus the great preserver of cosmological knowledge in this early period was the practice of computus, the science essential for ordering the ecclesiastical calendar. Literally thousands of medieval computus manuscripts survive, containing a pastiche of works covering such topics as the motions of the sun and moon and planets, the cause of eclipses, the divisions of time, the seasons, and the classical names and characteristics of the twelve winds. The computus book completed at the Benedictine monastery of Thorney in East Anglia in 1110 is a magnificent example, containing Bede's works on time, as well as numerous excerpts from other works. It is illustrated with dozens of diagrams and maps (see Figure 11).

Plato's universe was easily adapted to Christian philosophy. The moving intelligences of the heavenly bodies were transmuted into angels, and God, of course, became the ultimate prime mover. Plato's idea, echoed by Aristotle, that the spheres increased in 'honour' the further they were removed from the earth, found resonance for Christians in the image of ascent into the heavens and a celestial hierarchy, corresponding to the ideal earthly one. For centuries Christian philosophers continued to tinker with their cosmology, adding refinements and details, based on theology more than on observation. The six days of Creation described in Genesis were the framework for numerous works which outlined the unfolding of God's handiwork (see Figure 12). The *Hexameron* of St Ambrose, delivered as a series of homilies in 387, attempted to reconcile the principles of natural science with Scripture. If the two were in conflict, naturally the word of God prevailed. Plato's concept of the creation of the universe was true enough, but his assertion that it would last forever was clearly contradicted by statements made by Jesus in the Gospels. Ambrose also put an allegorical interpretation on geographical features. In *Paradise* he tells us that the Four Rivers which flow from the fountain of Paradise may be the Tigris, the Euphrates, the Nile and the Ganges, but they also represent the four cardinal virtues, while Paradise is in the East, because Christ is the 'rising sun'. One puzzle, the idea of the 'waters above the earth', was solved by simply adding another sphere, the crystalline sphere of solidified water. Erratic celestial phenomena, such

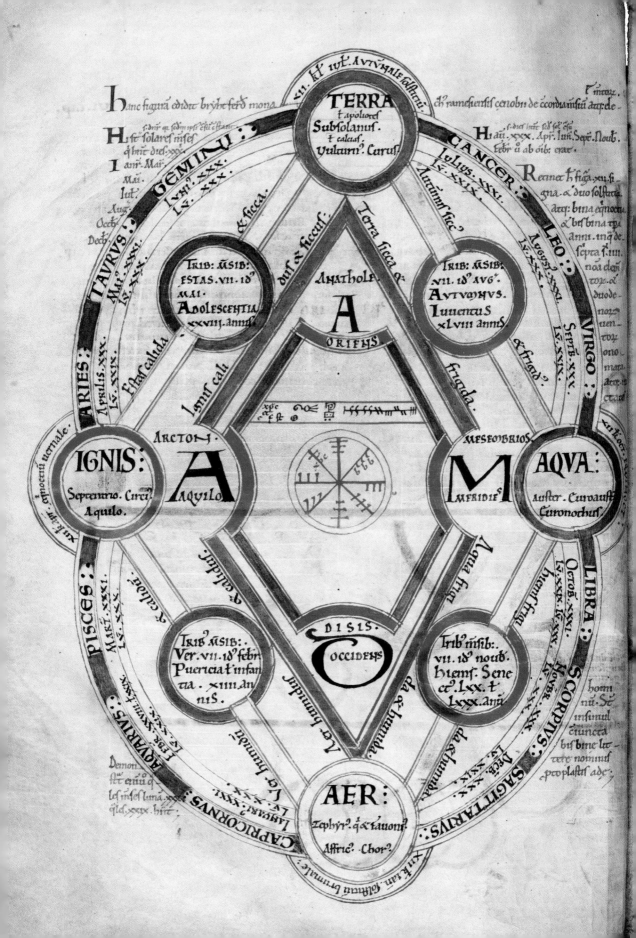

sedem in ysaia. tertium in zacharia. quartum in proverbiis. quintum eque in ysaia. Quod multi ignorantes apocriforum deliramenta sectantur, et hyberas nenias libris autenticis preferunt. Causas erroris non est meum exponere. Iudei prudenti factum dicunt consilio, ne ptolomeus unius dei cultor etiam apud hebreos duplicem divinitatem deprehenderet. Quos maxime idcirco faciebant, quia in platonis dogma cadere videbatur. Denique ubicumque sacratum aliquid scriptura testatur de patre et filio et spiritu sancto, aut aliter interpretati sunt, aut omnino tacuerunt, ut et regi satisfacerent, et archanum fidei non vulgarent. Et nescio quis primus auctor lxx cellulas alexandrie mendacio suo extruxerit, quibus divisi eadem scriptitarent, cum aristeus eiusdem ptolomei yperaspistes et multo post tempore iosephus nichil tale retulerint, sed in una basilica congregatos contulisse scribant, non prophetasse. Aliud est enim esse vatem, aliud esse interpretem. Ibi spiritus ventura predicit, hic eruditio et verborum copia ea que intelligit transfert. Nisi forte putandus est tullius economicum xenofontis et platonis pitagoram et demostenis pro ctesifonte afflatus rethorico spiritu transtulisse, aut aliter de eisdem libris per lxx interpretes, aliter per apostolos spiritus sanctus testimonia texuit, ut quod illi tacuerunt, hii scriptum esse mentiti sint. hic Quid igitur? Dampnamus veteres? Minime. Sed post priorum studia in domo domini quod possumus laboramus. Illi interpretati sunt ante adventum christi, et quod nesciebant dubiis protulere sententiis. Nos post passionem et resurrectionem eius non tam prophetiam quam historiam scribimus. Aliter enim audita, aliter visa narrantur. Quod melius intelligimus, melius et proferimus. Audi igitur emule, obtrectator ausculta. Non dampno, non reprehendo lxx, sed confidenter cunctis illis apostolos prefero. Per istorum os michi christus sonat, quos ante prophetas inter spiritualia

carismata positos lego, in quibus ultimum pene gradum interpretes tenent. Quid livore torqueris? Quid imperitorum animos contra me concitas? Sicubi in translatione tibi videor errare, interroga hebreos, diversarum urbium magistros consule. Quod illi habent de christo, tui codices non habent. Aliud est si contra se postea ab apostolis usurpata testimonia probaverunt, et emendatiora sunt exemplaria latina quam greca, greca quam hebrea. Verum hec contra invidos. Nunc te deprecor desideri karissime, ut quia me tantum opus subire fecisti et a genesi exordium capere, orationibus iuves quo possim eodem spiritu quo scripti sunt libri in latinum eos transferre sermonem.

explicit prologus

In principio — incipit liber bresith — creavit deus celum et terram. Terra autem erat inanis et vacua, et tenebre erant super faciem abyssi, et spiritus dei ferebatur super aquas. Dixitque deus: Fiat lux. Et facta est lux. Et vidit deus lucem quod esset bona, et divisit lucem a tenebris. Appellavitque lucem diem et tenebras noctem. Factumque est vespere et mane dies unus. Dixit quoque deus: Fiat firmamentum in medio aquarum, et dividat aquas ab aquis. Et fecit deus firmamentum, divisitque aquas que erant sub firmamento ab hiis que erant super firmamentum. Et factum est ita. Vocavitque deus firmamentum celum. Et factum est vespere et mane dies secundus. Dixit vero deus: Congregentur aque que sub celo sunt in locum unum, et appareat arida. Factumque est ita. Et vocavit deus aridam terram, congregationesque aquarum appellavit maria. Et vidit deus quod esset bonum, et ait: Germinet terra herbam virentem et facientem semen, et lignum pomiferum faciens fructum iuxta genus suum, cuius semen in semetipso sit super terram. Et factum est ita. Et protulit terra herbam virentem et facientem semen iuxta genus suum, lignumque

afferentem

as comets and meteors, were explained in a way that would preserve the ideal of the unchanging heavens.

The reign of Charlemagne (768–814) saw a new emphasis in western Europe on various intellectual projects, including the copying of numerous classical manuscripts and the founding of monastic libraries and schools, though there was little new development in the realm of cosmology. Despite Charlemagne's diplomatic contacts with his great contemporary, the caliph Hārūn al-Rashīd (786–809) in Baghdad, none of the scientific activity flourishing in the Islamic world at that time seems to have been transmitted to Europe. It was not until the twelfth century that western Europe gained access to the works of Aristotle and Ptolemy.

Figure 12. The days of creation as described in Genesis from the opening page of a Bible. MS Auct.D.5.14, fol. 4r (English, 14th century).

2

Science in the Islamic Regions

While Charlemagne's reign in Europe marked a period of increased cultural activity, the intellectual achievements at the court in Baghdad at the same time were considerably greater. In the year 750, the capital of the Islamic world moved from Damascus to Baghdad, which then became a centre for the study and translation of Greek medical and scientific writings and for the composition of the earliest Arabic treatises on these topics. Men of letters, religious scholars, poets, and scholars of all sorts enjoyed the patronage of the court in Baghdad, especially during the reigns of Hārūn al-Rashīd (786–809) and al-Ma'mūn (813–833). The Greek-to-Arabic translation movement that took place in Baghdad from the mid-eighth through the tenth century was the result of a sustained program subsidised publicly and privately by the élite, and produced translations of virtually the entire corpus of Greek science. These teachings were valued by a vigorous Islamic empire which sought ways of dealing with health problems, timekeeping requirements (determination of prayer times, calendric conversions, record keeping), mathematical calculations (surveying, geodesy), and astronomical needs. This heritage of scientific theory and practice, mingled with Persian, Indian, and Arab elements, was elaborated and expanded by a community of both Muslim and non-Muslim scholars speaking many languages—Greek, Syriac, Arabic, Persian, Hebrew—though Arabic remained the *lingua franca* and Islam the dominant faith.

While almost all the Greek scientific and philosophical writings were translated at this time, there is a notable exception: the writings of Plato. For reasons somewhat obscure, virtually all the writings of Aristotle were available to Arabic scholars but almost none of the Platonic dialogues. This stands in rather stark contrast to early medieval Europe where Plato was known, but Aristotle hardly at all.

Amongst the treatises rendered into Arabic were the *Elements* of Euclid, written in Alexandria around 300 BC; treatises on mechanics by Archimedes (*c*.287–212 BC); and the writings on astronomy, geography, astrology, harmonics, and optics by Ptolemy in the second century AD, also composed in Alexandria. Of Ptolemy's treatises, two figure most prominently for our purposes: the *Almagest*, and the *Geography*, though his treatise on astrology (generally known by its Greek title *Tetrabiblos* or 'Four Books') was also important.

Ptolemy's *Almagest* became the foundational text of mathematical astronomy and was to dominate all astronomical thought until the time of Copernicus and Galileo in the sixteenth and seventeenth centuries. The title by which it is known, *Almagest*, derives from the Arabic word *al-mijistī*, a contraction of the Arabic rendering of the Greek title *Megalē syntaxis* ('the Large System'). Using mathematical models, Ptolemy attempted to construct a theoretical cosmos which would explain the true order beneath the seeming irregularities of the movements of the heavens. *The Almagest* was technically challenging (still true today) and Ptolemy's ideas were spread mostly by means of commentaries written by adept readers, such as al-Farghānī (d. after 861) and John of Sacrobosco (early thirteenth century). The book covered solar and lunar motion, the theory of eclipses based on almost 1,000 years of observations, and geometric explanations of the orbits of the planets. A catalogue of the 1,022 so-called 'fixed' stars included specific coordinates and magnitudes assigned to each star, as well as their organization into 48 constellations in human or animal form.

Non-mathematical astronomy, however, had an even wider audience. Interest in the stars, and the changing course of the sun and moon through them, is manifest in all early societies. The Qur'ān (3:8 and 4:4) remarks that the Creator made the stars to adorn the lowest heaven and to be useful to mankind as guides for night-journeys, both across the trackless desert and at sea: 'It is He Who maketh the stars for you, that you may guide yourselves with their help, through the dark spaces of land and sea' (6:97). Caravans travelled at night through the scorching deserts of Arabia, and so it is not surprising that early Arabs would have closely observed the movements of the stars and planets overhead and learned to use them for guidance.

The use of stars for navigation at sea is suggested as early as the voyage of Odysseus. On leaving Calypso's isle, Odysseus, Homer tells us:

Figure 13. The constellation Orion as seen in the sky (left) and on a celestial globe (right), from *The Book of Constellations* by al-al-Ṣūfī (d. 986). MS. Marsh 144, pp. 325–6 (dated 400H [1009]; 12th-century?).

never closed his eyes in sleep, but kept them on the Pleiades, or watched Boötes slowly set, or the Great Bear, nicknamed the Wain, which always wheels round in the same place and looks across at Orion the Hunter with a wary eye. It was this constellation, the only one which never bathes in the Ocean's Stream, that the wise goddess Calypso had told him to keep on his left hand as he made his way across the sea.[4]

Nevertheless, travelling by ship at night was a dangerous business, made the more so by the lack of lighting techniques for scanning the waters ahead. The introduction of the magnetic compass in the late twelfth or early thirteenth century was a great boon to sailors out at sea on cloudy nights, and played a role in the development of sea charts. The majority of ships, east and west, however, sailed in daylight and depended on the guidance of experienced pilots familiar with the requirements of ports, winds, and the changing position of the sun at given latitudes. Sources prior to the fifteenth century say nothing about

how sailors navigated, except for vague references to written lists of harbours and an occasional noting of the position of the pole star. In 1460 Ibn Mājid recorded in detail sailing techniques used in the Indian Ocean, employing a magnetic compass and the measurement of the altitudes of star-groups called 'lunar mansions'. True astronomical navigation based on precise observations of the sun and stars did not develop until the late sixteenth century. It is worth recalling that Christopher Columbus was extremely sketchy on the use of the quadrant and managed to find his way to America and back several times using only a compass, log and line, and his own acute observation of the sea.

There was great interest in illustrating constellations of stars and in using the appearance of prominent stars to predict seasonal changes. The most important guide to constellations in the Islamic world was *The Book of the Constellations of the Fixed Stars* by 'Abd al-Raḥmān al-Ṣūfī (d. 986), a court astronomer in Isfahan in Iran. The idea of constructing a physical model to represent the heavens appears to have first arisen in Greek antiquity in the sixth century BC. The stars were perceived—as indeed they still are by anyone who looks up into the night sky—as though attached to the inside of a hollow sphere enclosing and rotating about the earth. Consequently, the earliest attempts to represent celestial phenomena in a model were by means of a celestial globe. The earth was imagined at the centre of the globe, while the stars were placed on the surface of the globe. The resulting model presented the stars from the viewpoint of an observer placed outside the sphere of stars, with the effect that the relative positions of the stars are the reverse of their appearance when viewed from the surface of the earth. It was for this reason that in his book al-Ṣūfī presented two images of each constellation, one a mirror image of the other (see Figure 13).

Most of the classical forty-eight constellation outlines, which are merely devices for aiding in the location and recognition of a star, will be familiar to readers acquainted with modern star maps; one exception is the large southern constellation of the ship (Argo Navis) which is no longer recognized today as a constellation but has been broken up into several smaller units. In classical and medieval descriptions there are relatively few constellations in the southern region (one large area is completely devoid of stars), for this part of the sky remained unmapped until the geographical explorations of the sixteenth century.

Figure 14 *right*. The constellation Cassiopeia as seen on a globe, with the Arab constellation of a camel drawn over her, from *The Book of Constellations* by al-Sūfī. MS. Hunt. 212, folio 40b (1170–1 [566 H]).

Figure 15 *far right*. The constellation Cassiopeia, from the *Poetica Astronomica* of Hyginus (1st cent. BC). MS. Canon Class. Lat. 179, fol. 34v (15th century).

Figure 16 *below*. The constellation Perseus, from the *Poetica Astronomica* of Hyginus (1st cent. BC). MS. Canon. Class. Lat. 179, fol. 35v (15th century).

Al-Sūfī also described the constellations used in pre-Islamic Arabia and related them to their classical Greek counterparts. In one of the rare copies to illustrate these Bedouin constellations, the pre-Islamic Arab constellation of a camel is depicted above the classical constellation of Cassiopeia (see Figure 14).

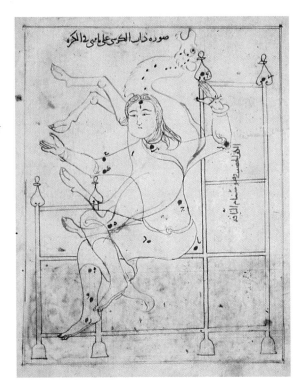

In the Arabic treatises, the Greek mythological prototypes for these constellations (Orion, Perseus, Andromeda, etc.) were transformed, with the garments, hair-styles, and jewellery changed to conform to the fashions and artistic conventions at the time and place of production. So, the lion's skin which according to Greek tradition hung over the hunter Orion in his constellation was converted in the Islamic world into a very long sleeve.

In the medieval European tradition, we can see a similar adjustment to time and place in the illustrations of constellations. The popular Latin astronomical poem *Poetica astronomica*, attributed to Hyginus (first century BC), supplied the myths behind the classical constellation figures, and copies were often copiously illustrated (see Figures 15 and 16). Groups of constellations also decorated the pages of astronomical miscellanies

Asiepia sedens in siliquastro collocata est: cuius sedilis et ipsius pedes casiepie positi in ipsa circuductione circuli qui atthicos uocatur effigies autem corporis ad estiuum circulum puenit. quem capite & dextra manu tang. hanc ppe media diuidit circulus is q lacte appellat praxie cephei signum collocata. Hec occidens cum scorpione capite cum sedili rursipina ferri perspicitur: Exoriri autem cum sagittario. huius in capite stella dicitur una. in utroq. humero una. in mamilla dextra clara una. in lumbis magna una in sinistro femore duas. in genu una in pede ipsius dextro una. in quadrato quo stella disformatur una. in utrisq. singule clarius ceteris lucentes. hic igit est oio stellarum ous tredecim.

Virgo que et iusticia appellat' ht stellā in capite obscuram ualde·1·Jn vna quaqᷓ ala·1· Jn singlis humis sigtas. Jn vnoqᷓ cubito·1· Jn singlis manibᷓ sigtas·Jn penula uestimti·6· Jn vnoqᷓ pede·1· Sunt oms·19·

Leo ht stellas in capite·3· Jn cuuce·z· Jn ptore·7 in dorso·3· Jn summitate caude splendida·1· sb pectore·z· Jn antioze pede splendida·1· sūt oms·13·

Auriga ht stellā in capite·1· Jn utroqᷓ humo·1· si ea est clarioz que in sinistᷓ humo ē·Jn utroqᷓ cubito·1· Jn dextra manu·1· Jn summitate mani sinistre·z· Jn sñ ipo brachio ædulos·z·7 in utroqᷓ cedulo stella·1· Sunt oms·10·

Gemini ob oz q ex dic a cant ht stellā in capite splendidā·1· Jn utroqᷓ humo splendida·1· Jn utroqᷓ genu·1· ut oms·q· Alt v ht in capite stella splēdicā·1· Jn humio sinistᷓ·1· per singla femora·1· Jn dorso·3· ut oms·A· Jnt utroqᷓ·12·

Taurus ht stellas in utroqᷓ cornu·1· Jn fronte·z· p singlos oclos·1· Jn nare·1· hec ā stelle pliades 7 ugilie nno 7 ubucle dnt· Jn utroqᷓ genu·1· Jn collo·z· Jn dorso·3· ex qbᷓ no uissima splendida ē· Jn uter ·1· Jn pectore·1· Sunt oms·16·

Cancer ht stellas splendidas ni tcio·q· Jn dextᷓs pedibᷓ p singlos·1· Jn sinistᷓ pmo·z·7 in sinistᷓ tcio·1· Jn qᷓto·1· Jn oze·1· Jn dextro labio·3· Jn sinistᷓ·z· Sunt oms·18·

Cepheus ht in capite stellas splendidas·z· Et in dextᷓ manu splendida·1· Jn utroqᷓ humio·1· Jn zona·3· Jn dextᷓ latere extimsuso sup illu·1· Jn sinistᷓ genu·z· Jn summitate pedū·q· Sunt oms·21·

36

(Figure 17). It should be noted, however, that in medieval Western drawings the stars are only casually placed and there is no attempt to number them or give a precise indication of their positions, as al-Sūfī undertook to do. On the other hand, the Arabic and Persian treatises do not supply the mythologies for the constellation figures, a favourite topic in ancient and medieval European writings on astronomy for the general audience.

In pre-Islamic Arabia another system of categorizing stars was devised, employing star groups smaller than constellations. These were 'lunar mansions', whose risings and settings were thought important in predicting rain and other meteorological phenomena (see Figure 9, where they occupy the outmost band, and Figure 18). Twenty-eight

Figure 17 *left*. The constellations Virgo, Gemini, Cancer, Leo, Auriga (the Charioteer), Taurus, and Cepheus, from an astronomical miscellany written in Bayeux c. 1268–74. MS. Laud misc. 644, fol. 8v.

Figure 18 *diagram below and illustrated overleaf*. A diagram of the skies, with Earth at the centre surrounded by a ring of 28 'lunar mansions' and a ring of 48 classical constellations, with the 12 zodiacal signs at the periphery. MS. Arab. c. 90, fols. 2b-3a (12th-13th century).

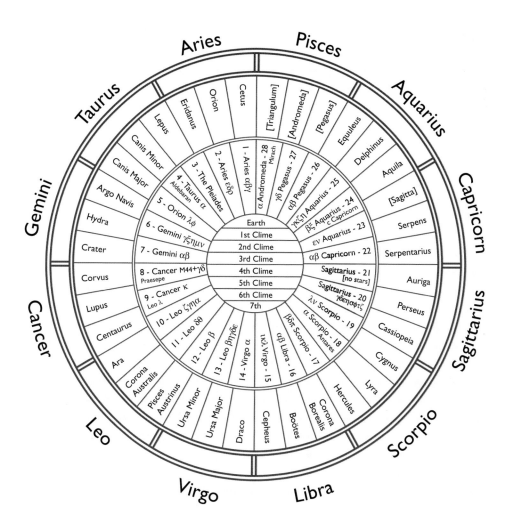

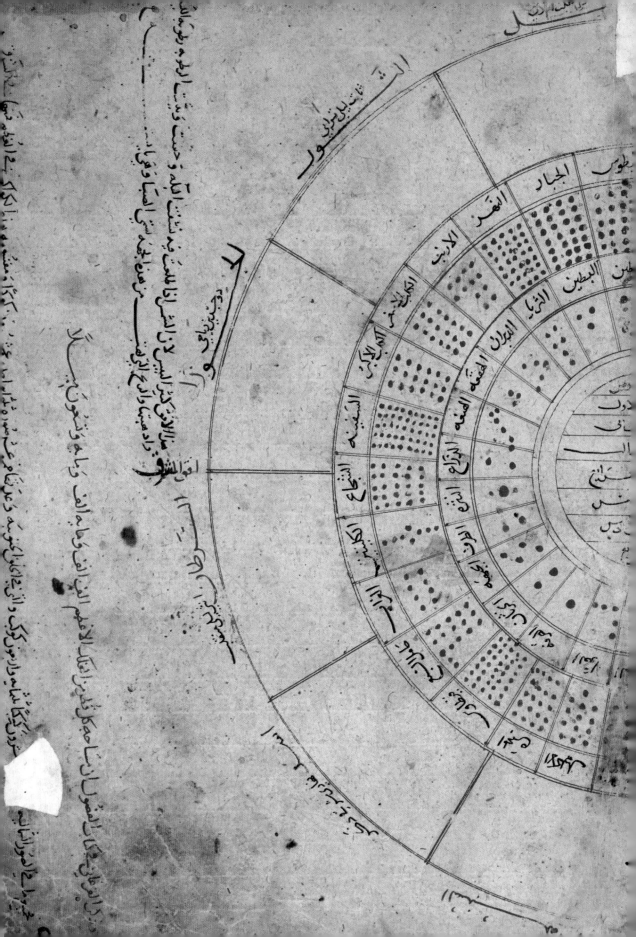

Figure 19. Talismanic designs of 14 'lunar mansions', from an Arabic miscellany compiled for the Mongol ruler of Baghdad, Sulṭān Aḥmad, who ruled 1382–1410. MS. Bodl. Or. 133, fol. 27b.

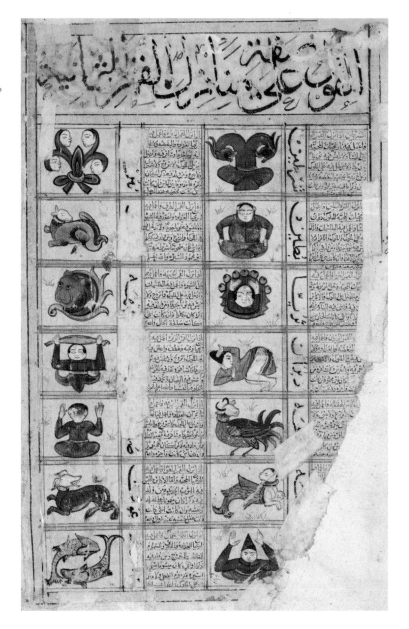

star-groups were distinguished, corresponding in number to the twenty-eight phases of the lunar cycle. The open star cluster of the Pleiades is the most conspicuous of the 'lunar mansions'. In about 1460, Ibn Mājid described the use of these star-groups for navigation in the Indian Ocean, but they were of interest not just to astronomers or navigators or pastoral peoples forecasting seasonal changes—they also played a prominent role in astrology and magic, both in Islamic regions and in the medieval West. Talismanic designs were sometimes associated with them, magnificently illustrated in an Arabic miscellany

compiled for the Mongol ruler of Baghdad, Sulṭan Ahmad (ruled 1382–1410). In Figure 19, fourteen of the 'lunar mansions' are depicted, not as star-groups but as talismanic images. The appearance of the Pleiades was traditionally associated with disease, so the design associated with it (the third down in the right-hand column of Figure 19) could be used as a powerful protective amulet.

Planets, as well as stars, were thought to exert direct physical influence on earthly events, and astrologers gave particular attention to the position of the sun and other planets as they moved through the zodiac, the narrow band of the heavens containing the pathway of the sun. Each zodiacal sign occupies 30° of the circle of the zodiac, and each is divided into three 10°-segments (or decans) over which a particular planet rules: for example, the sign of Pisces is governed by Saturn in the first 10° segment, Jupiter in the second, and Mars in the third. Occasionally, as in Figure 20, these associations were illustrated allegorically.

Extraordinary celestial events were also of importance. The appearance of comets, for example, was considered to be especially ominous. Comets are occasionally depicted in illustrations of historical events, most notably in the Bayeux Tapestry where the appearance of the comet presaged the Norman invasion of 1066. Nevertheless, illustrated essays on the topic are exceedingly rare in the preserved medieval literature. An anonymous early eleventh-century Arabic treatise, *The Book of Curiosities of the Sciences and Marvels for the Eyes* (hereafter shortened for convenience to the *Book of Curiosities*) has two illustrated chapters devoted to comets (see Figure 21) with associated events as in the following example:

> If the comet known as 'The Lamp' appears in the east, it is a sign of a great famine in that region, fires, civil war, bloodshed, and abundance of thunderbolts. It also foretells flames of no known cause destroying forests and inhabited regions, setting ablaze the mansions of kings and especially those which they have erected for themselves, corrupting the fruits, drying up the springs and the rivers and bringing heat to the horizons. And there is a multitude of shooting stars. If this comet appears in the west and

Figure 20. The sign of Pisces (represented by a cross-legged man next to a fish) with anthropomorphised representations of three planets ruling a segment of the sign: (right to left) Saturn, Jupiter, and Mars; from an Arabic miscellany compiled for the Mongol ruler of Baghdad, Sulṭan Ahmad, who ruled 1382–1410. MS. Bodl. Or. 133, fol. 22b.

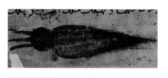

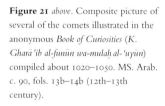

the south, it is a sign of a civil war erupting in the midst of the region in which it appeared, bringing cruelty, wars and the corruption of crops in the west. This is what it looks like.[5]

Europeans, such as Robert Grosseteste (1168-1253), agreed that comets were bad news, but struggled with an additional problem—what was such an obviously unstable body doing in the immutable celestial sphere? Grosseteste, in his reflections on the comet of 1196-97, surmised that the comet was made of the terrestrial element, fire, that had somehow strayed into the upper regions.

While comets gave rise to observation and speculation, the stars and sun in relation to the horizon yielded valuable information on time-keeping and navigation. The instrument which made this possible was the astrolabe, the most complex of medieval astronomical instruments whose beauty and intricacy have made it a favourite subject for illustration (Figure 22). The planispheric or flat astrolabe used a mathematical method called 'stereographic projection' to represent on a flat surface the stars as positioned on the celestial globe. It is a two-dimensional model of the heavens in relation to the local horizon (Figure 23).

The astrolabe was a Hellenistic invention, but its design and production were perfected in the Islamic world. Early medieval compilers of biographies and histories often interlaced their accounts with charming anecdotes of doubtful authenticity. A particularly delightful example is

Figure 21 *above*. Composite picture of several of the comets illustrated in the anonymous *Book of Curiosities* (*K. Gharā'ib al-funūn wa-mulaḥ al-'uyūn*) compiled about 1020–1050. MS. Arab. c. 90, fols. 13b–14b (12th–13th century).

Figure 22 *right*. Two seated astronomers, the one on the right holding an astrolabe, the other a celestial globe (labelled *sfera*), from the *Experimentarius* of Bernard Silvestri. MS. Digby 46, fol. 8v. (English, 13th century).

the account of the origin of the astrolabe given in the thirteenth century by the Syrian bibliographer Ibn Khallikān. He related that 'it is said' Ptolemy invented the astrolabe by accident. He was out riding his horse one day and dropped the celestial globe he was carrying, whereupon his mount stepped on it and crushed it. And so the astrolabe was created.[6]

Although the flat astrolabe could be used only at a few pre-defined latitudes, it was more portable than a celestial globe and included a sighting device for making observations. By observing the positions of the sun or the stars, the astrolabe could be used for telling the time for prayers, for determining geographical orientation, and for calculations involved in casting horoscopes. It quickly became the most important astronomical and astrological instrument in the Islamic world from the eighth century. From the middle of the tenth century knowledge of it spread to Europe, so that by 1092 an astrolabe was being employed in England during an eclipse. The astrolabe, however, was not sufficiently precise for detailed astronomical observations of stellar and planetary coordinates. For those purposes other larger, more precise instruments were employed, such as a parallactic ruler, the dioptra, large quadrants (instruments graduated through an arc of 90° for taking angular measurements), and observational armillary spheres. The astrolabe, moreover, was highly impractical, if not downright useless, for navigation on board ship. A simplified, weighted form, known as the mariner's astrolabe, was developed in Europe in the sixteenth century for use at sea, while the quadrant was widely known in Europe by the fourteenth century. Later in the sixteenth century a plane-mounted astrolabe became a common tool for land surveying.

Figure 23. Planispheric astrolabe made in 1081-2 (474 H) in the Spanish city of Guadalajara by Muḥammad ibn Saʿīd al-Ṣabbān, known as Ibn Mashshāṭ al-Saraqusṭī al-Asṭurlābī ('the astrolabe-maker of Saragossa'). Oxford, Museum of the History of Science, Inv. no. 52473.

3

Twelfth–Century European Renaissance

It is said that Gerard of Cremona (*c*.1114–87) went to Toledo
specifically seeking Ptolemy's *Almagest*, the astronomical masterwork of
the second century of our era. He had heard of this book but had been
unable to obtain a copy. In Islamic Spain he discovered such a wealth
of books on all topics that he remained for some forty years, directing a
small army of translators. Among the seventy or eighty works which
were thus brought to the attention of the West were not only the
Almagest but also Euclid's *Elements*, medical treatises by Galen, and
Aristotle's *Physics, On the Heavens, Meteorology,* and *On Generation and
Corruption*. In addition there were important texts by Arabic mathema-
ticians and scientists, such as the algebra of al-Khwārazmī (d. *c*.847) and
the *Canon of Medicine* of Ibn Sīnā (d. 1037), known to Europeans as
Avicenna. The translation from Arabic into Latin continued into the
next century until nearly all of Aristotle's works were available in
Latin. Contact with Islamic scientists also brought the astrolabe, a
device so novel and useful that it became practically the centre of a
cult. The philosophers Abelard (d. 1142) and Héloise (d. 1164) even
named their son 'Astrolabe'. Just before composing *The Canterbury
Tales* Geoffrey Chaucer produced in 1391 an entire treatise on the
astrolabe for the instruction of his ten-year old son, Lowys (Lewis).
The astrolabe was so closely allied in the popular imagination with
astronomy that it often appeared in paintings to indicate an astronomer
(see Figure 22).

The rediscovery of Aristotle in the West during the twelfth century
introduced a philosopher who had accepted the basic Platonic cosmic
structure, with some modifications and much more detail, though his
approach was less abstract and more materialistic. All events in his
opinion must have a material cause. The ultimate cause of all motions
was the 'Prime Mover', which Aristotle placed on the outermost

sphere of the universe (see Figure 1). But he also gave each of the planetary spheres its own 'Unmoved Mover', leading to charges of pantheism against his works in the early thirteenth century. Medieval Christians were also horrified to discover that he postulated an eternal universe, not a created one.[7] The universities banned Aristotle's works several times and in 1231 Pope Gregory IX appointed a commission to purge them of pagan material. This editing was never done, and by the end of the thirteenth century the unexpurgated Aristotle had secured a central place in the curriculum. Muslim thinkers had of course been aware of Aristotle's view that the world was eternal and time without an end, but most had simply relegated that particular idea to a list of those considered incorrect, as when al-Bīrūnī in the early eleventh century wrote 'Other people, besides, hold this foolish belief that *time* has no *terminus* at all.'[8]

In his *Almagest*, Ptolemy had added numerous refinements to the Platonic-Aristotelian world picture which helped coordinate theory and observation. In order to track the paths of the planets he altered the many earth-centred spheres governing their motion to epicycles, or eccentric circles, not centred on the earth. The conflicting views on planetary spheres led to serious disagreement in the Middle Ages, an argument which was to rage up to the time of Copernicus. As for Ptolemy's *Geography,* it remained unknown in the West until the early fifteenth century, though, like other Greek scientific tracts, it was available to Arabic scholars from the ninth century.

The recovery of Greek works, as well as the wealth of Arabic commentaries and treatises which were also translated, was a tremendous boost to the theory and practice of science in the West. The coincidental founding and growth of the universities in the West provided an important institutional base for the propagation of new ideas, one of the most stimulating of which was the idea of making one's own observations instead of relying blindly on authority. The detailed astronomical observations, made in both the Islamic and Christian worlds, were eventually to undermine the Ptolemaic system and lead to the Copernican Revolution.

4

Microcosm/Macrocosm

Plato had poetically described the parallels between the human body and the universe in the *Timaeus*. Man was a 'minor mundus', a little world, reflecting in both body and soul the structure of the cosmos. The four elements which made up the universe went to compose the human body, manifesting themselves in the form of the humours or fluids: blood, phlegm, yellow bile, and black bile. The humours produced the four temperaments, which were sanguine, phlegmatic, choleric, and melancholic. An imbalance among the humours was the principal cause of disease. The great Greek physician, Galen (129 – 210), following Hippocrates, expounded this concept in his works on medicine, which were handed down to a grateful and receptive Middle Ages. Ailing individuals were diagnosed and purged of the offending humour, as in the practice of blood-letting. If the body of the human being reflected the universe, the idea of influences was a natural step. Parts of the body were under the dominion of the various signs of the zodiac, and innumerable tables and charts were made during the Middle Ages to show when it was most propitious to undergo the appropriate medical treatment (see Figure 4).

Diagrams of correspondences carried the connection still further. The elements were linked not only to the humours, but to the four qualities of matter (hot, cold, wet, dry), the seasons, and the ages of man. The great diagram made by Byrhtferth in the tenth century also includes the cardinal directions, the signs of the zodiac, the twelve winds, the months of the year, and the solstices and equinoxes (see Figure 11). To complete the picture, the initial letters of the cardinal directions in Greek spell out the name of Adam, the first human being.

Early Christian thinkers, such as Augustine, had condemned the practice of astrology, seeing it as too closely connected with the

worship of the deified planets and as a threat to the Christian concept of free will. Astrology did not disappear, however, and was in fact productive, in both the Islamic and Latin world, of careful observation and recording of astronomical phenomena. The Toledan Tables of geographical coordinates, compiled in the eleventh century by al-Zarqēllo, were based on extensive astronomical observations, though their primary interest was in casting nativities, or birth horoscopes. It was acceptable Christian belief to think of 'tendencies' inherent in the positions of the stars and planets, so long as human beings retained the ultimate responsibility of decision-making. In the twelfth century the new interest in science, spurred by contact with the Islamic world and the influx of Greek works, led to an increased enthusiasm for astrology.

Figure 24. Map showing planetary and zodiacal influences on different territories (south at the top), from John Ashenden's *Summa judicialis*. MS. Bodl. 369, fol. 68r (English, 14th century).

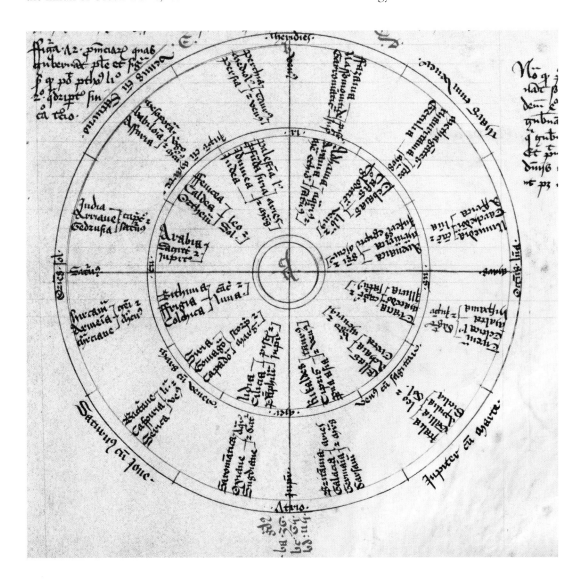

If man is part of the universe, a better understanding of the universe would surely lead to a deeper understanding of man. Among the works of Ptolemy brought to the attention of the West was his *Tetrabiblos*, a treatise on astrology which put forth the idea of planetary dominance of different portions of the earth. Some of these observations became commonplace: for example, England was under the dominion of the moon and thus its citizens were inclined to be changeable, incapable of rational argument, and prone to wander from home. A map made by the Oxford scholar, John of Ashenden (mid-fourteenth century), shows the territories arranged according to the planets and zodiac signs which rule them (Figure 24). The position of the heavenly bodies also accounted for earthquakes, floods and other events such as pestilence, war, and an outbreak of thievery. Ashenden named the Arabic masters Albumasar (Abū Ma'shar, 787—886) and Hali ('Ali ibn 'Abbās al-Majūsī, d. 994) as his principal sources. Astrology continued to be practiced enthusiastically throughout the medieval period, and many important people had their horoscopes cast as a matter of course. In the seventeenth century, at the height of the Scientific Revolution, Johannes Kepler, the imperial mathematician at Prague, was distracted from his work on the *New Astronomy* by the task of casting horoscopes for distinguished visitors at the court of Rudolph II.

5

The Geographical Inheritance from Antiquity

The Greeks and Romans were known to have made maps of the world. One of the earliest unambiguous references to such maps occurs in Herodotus's *Histories*. The envoy from Miletus has come to Sparta in 499 BC to beg for her aid in support of the Ionian cities, now in revolt against the Persian Empire. He presents 'a bronze tablet, whereupon the whole circuit of the earth was engraved, with all its seas and rivers'. Expounding on the map, he describes the rich kingdoms between the Ionian coast and the Persian capital of Susa, all of which will lie open to the looting Greek armies. Cleomenes, the Spartan king, viewing with suspicion this cartographic display, places his finger on the crucial point and exclaims: 'Milesian stranger, quit Sparta before sunset. This is no good proposal that you make to the Laedaemonians, to conduct them a distance of three months' journey from the sea.'[9]

As the Romans expanded their empire to the limits of the known world, one might have expected a world map as a natural outcome. Indeed some scholars have suggested that the Romans could not have governed their empire effectively without the use of maps. Pliny the Elder (d. 79 AD) described a monumental map of the Empire, which was designed by Marcus Vipsanius Agrippa and set up in a public space in Rome in 12 BC. There is some controversy as to whether it was a map or an inscription, as we do not know exactly what form it took. Throughout his *Natural History* Pliny notes dimensions and distances drawn from this 'plan of the world'.[10]

Unfortunately no remnants of these maps have survived. The world maps which we do have from ancient Rome are those copied into manuscripts from the nineth century on as illustrations for classical works, such as the histories of Sallust (86–34 BC) and the epic poem on the civil war between Pompey and Caesar composed by Lucan (39–65

Figure 25. Map from Sallust's *History of the Jugurthine Wars,* with the lion's share of the place-names in Africa and, unusually, west at the top. MS. Rawl. G. 44, fol. 17v (Flemish, 11th century).

AD). These maps (see Figure 25) are simple and abstract, based on the form called the T-O map, and show the known world as a circle with three continents. Asia, the largest of the continents, is usually placed at the top of the map, with Europe and Africa dividing the space below. Three bodies of water—the Mediterranean Sea, the Nile, and the river Don—divide the landmasses. To this simple design artists sometimes added refinements, such as the four cardinal directions or the twelve winds around the edge. A few cities or countries might be put in the picture to dress it up, such as in the maps illustrating Sallust's history of

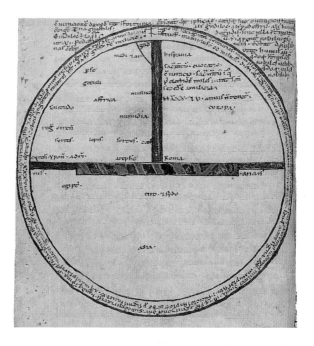

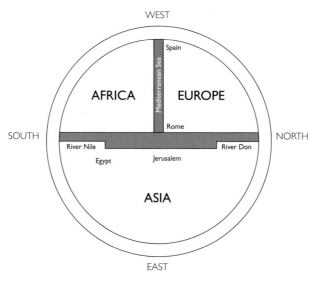

a colonial war in Africa where a dozen places are added, including the puzzling designation of the 'Medes, Armenians, and Persians', relics of Hercules's disbanded army, who continued to appear on such maps throughout the Middle Ages.

Some T–O diagrams were made into 'list-maps', with each continental space containing a list of the most important places therein (Figure 26). Others added simple geographical features and place-names, more or less in accord with their actual location.

Another model which survives from antiquity is the zonal map found in Macrobius's fifth-century *Commentary* on the *Dream of Scipio*. In it Scipio Africanus the Younger is transported into the heavens where he sees the spirit of his adoptive grandfather, Scipio Africanus the Elder (see Figure 10). Cicero's work, in which this 'dream' is first recounted, is mostly a reflection on political morality but it includes Scipio's vision of the earth below and the surrounding heavens. Macrobius, writing 400 years later, was mainly interested in the astronomy and geography, and accompanying his *Commentary* is a set of diagrams including a

Figure 26. T-O diagram containing lists of place-names grouped by continent, from Bede's *De temporum ratione*. MS. Canon Misc. 560, fol. 3r (11th century).

Figure 27. Zone map from Macrobius, *Commentary on the Dream of Scipio,* showing the five zones of the eastern hemisphere. MS. d'Orville 77, fol. 100r (German, 11th century).

world map (Figure 27). Here the eastern hemisphere is shown, with the earth divided into five climatic zones, mirroring the divisions of the heavens. The known world, confined to the northern temperate zone, was squeezed into one-fifth of the map's circular space and was generally depicted with only a few identifiable geographical features.

Macrobian maps show a parallel continent in the southern temperate zone, and his text describes a similar arrangement in the unknown Western hemisphere, though this is not pictured. The central torrid zone is usually described as uninhabitable and impassable, and the two polar or frigid zones are equally uninviting. The three hypothetical continents posed a problem for Christian thinkers. Even if they were willing to believe such lands existed, they did not think they could possibly be inhabited. In the *City of God* Augustine (d. 430) dismissed such an idea as mere 'scientific conjecture': If all men were descended from Adam and the intervening ocean was impassable, how then could these lands have been populated? When these maps were adapted into other manuscripts, they sometimes displayed new features, such as the movement of the tides and ocean currents around the globe, but they did not lend themselves to much geographic detail.[11]

The Greeks produced a number of geographical texts, many of these naturally being theoretical. To them we owe the division of the earth into the zones described above, as well as the greater refinement of the division of the inhabited portion into narrower regions or 'climes', each distinguished by its longest day being one half hour longer or shorter than the region immediately below or above. In Ptolemy's maps, 'climes' were an important organizing feature and continued to be used in the Islamic mapping tradition. Although the concept was known and passed on in geographical texts, 'climes' rarely appeared on western European maps until the revival of Ptolemy in the fifteenth century. An exception is the map by the Spaniard Petrus Alfonsi (1062–1120), which is the earliest recorded European map to show the seven 'climes' or regions of the inhabited world, and is certainly the result of Arab influence (Figure 28). Petrus, a Spanish Jew who

Figure 28. World map with 7 climes (above) and a diagram of the cosmos (below), from *Dialogi Moyse Judaeo* be Petrus Alfonsi (11th cent.). MS. Laud misc. 356, fol. 120r (French, early 14th century).

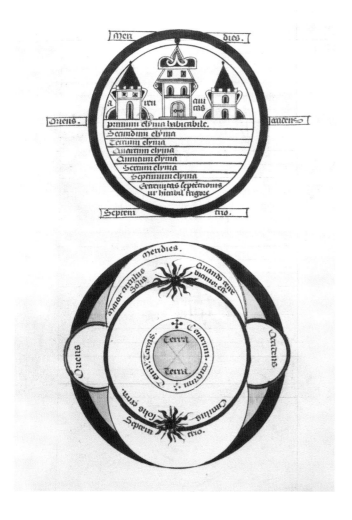

converted to Christianity around 1106, put the map in his *Dialogi contra Judaeos*, where he discusses the rationality of Christianity and the cosmos. South is at the top, Arabic-style, with the first 'clime' being the band beneath the three buildings that appear to sit on the Equator. Those buildings are labelled *Aren civitas* ('City of Aren'), the name of a mythical town of Hindu origin said to be on the meridian which bisects the inhabited world. Beneath the circular world map is a diagram of the cosmos showing the sun revolving about the earth at the centre, with south again at the top.

It was also the Greeks who first performed the calculations which determined the circumference of the earth, by estimating the length of a degree of latitude. After some false starts, Eratosthenes (third century BC) arrived at a conclusion amazingly close to what we know today. As sailors and travellers, the Greeks also accumulated some experiential data, gathered into coastal descriptions called *periploi* (literally 'circum-navigations') giving landmarks, directions, and distances between ports and between islands and the mainland. Several of them are preserved, dating from the fourth century BC to the fifth century AD. They are valuable sources for our knowledge of early coastal travel around the Mediterranean, the Black Sea, and the Indian Ocean, though no maps accompany any of these *periploi*.

The greatest of all Greek travellers was Alexander the Great (356–323 BC). A letter purported to be from him to Aristotle set forth the wonders he had seen, and it circulated throughout the Middle Ages, along with popular accounts of his exploits. To the core narrative of Alexander's already amazing adventures were added fantastic ones, in which he descended beneath the sea in a submarine and flew through the air in a chariot pulled by griffons. Illustrators of medieval manu-scripts delighted in illustrating these adventures, and he was depicted consulting the oracle tree in the Far East (see Figure 29) and confining the savage tribes of Gog and Magog, the mythical enemies of civiliza-tion who dwelt in the far north-east of the inhabitable world (see Figure 30). The barrier that he constructed to keep out Gog and Magog shows up repeatedly on medieval maps, both Western and Islamic (see Figures 39, 40, and 41 below).

The Romans were adept at surveying and road-building, activities which usually require maps, and a surveyors' manual and some mapped surveys do survive. Several land itineraries or route-lists also exist, most notably the Antonine Itinerary, composed in the late third century AD,

Figure 29. Alexander is shown interrogating the talking tree, which rebukes him for his lust of conquest and prophesies his death in a distant land; from the Persian epic *Shāhnāmah* by Firdawsī (d. 1020). MS. Ouseley Add.176, fol. 311b (Shiraz, c. 1430).

Figure 30. The construction of the barrier against Gog and Magog, from a Persian poem concerned with the life of Alexander the Great. MS. Elliot 340, fol. 80a (Bukhara, 1553 [960H]).

apparently for an imperial tour. The itinerary is a simple, though exhaustive, list of place-names with the distances between them. None of the early itineraries are illustrated, but there is an interesting road map, the Peutinger Scroll, bequeathed to us in a medieval copy of the twelfth or thirteenth century. Long and narrow, its length is about twenty times its height (675 cm long and 34 cm high). Because of its extraordinary shape, the north-south distances are greatly compressed while the east-west distances are much too long. The westernmost panel is lost, but in its original state it extended from Britain to China. The map includes distances, in the variety of measures used in the ancient world (leagues, stades, miles, parasangs), as well as symbols for towns, bridges, and bath-houses. While it shows Roman staging posts, no military installations are indicated on it, and its purpose is a subject of debate. Fragments also survive of a monumental map of the city of Rome carved in marble and originally mounted in the Forum.

6

Medieval Western Geography

In geography, as in astronomy, medieval Europe inherited from the classical world a small fraction of what it had produced. The lengthy description of the world in Pliny's *Natural History* was boiled down in the third century AD by Solinus, who unerringly selected the most marvellous and least precise of Pliny's observations, and indeed the title of his book was *Collection of Marvels* (*Collectanea Rerum Memorabilium*). To him the Middle Ages owed its extensive knowledge of the monstrous races of human beings who lived on the edges of the known world: people with one-eye or a single foot, those with no heads or with enormous ears, and those who devoured their parents in ceremonious feasting, produced children at the age of five, lived in caves, and had indiscriminate sexual relations (see Figure 31). Pliny's text was to disappear almost entirely from the medieval world, although Isidore seems to have had a treasured copy in seventh-century Spain, putting some of Pliny's material into his encyclopaedia, *The Etymologies*. As for the geographical works of Pomponius Mela (d. AD 42), Strabo (64 BC–21 AD), and Ptolemy, the West would have to wait until the Renaissance to read them.

The Bible contributed several crucial elements to the shaping of the European medieval world view, including Paradise, which was believed to have a real existence on the earth but in an inaccessible location in the East. In some interpretations it was surrounded by a ring of fire guarded by an angel with a flaming sword. Others theorized that it was on an island or on a mountain so high that it had escaped the great flood. Another concept, derived from Genesis, was that the Tigris, Euphrates, Ganges, and Nile all flowed from a single fountain in Paradise. The Greeks had already speculated on the idea of a single source for the great rivers of the East, though Aristotle had scoffed at it and the sources of these rivers remained unknown for

centuries. The 'Rivers of Paradise' provided a framework for world maps, which was somewhat problematic: if Paradise were in the East (as the Bible says) and is shut off from the fallen race of humanity, how do the rivers get from there to here? Honorius Augustodunensis (*c*.1098–1140) tacked the subject bravely in his *Imago Mundi*. The fountain is the source of the rivers, he writes, but once they leave Paradise, they flow in underground passages to reach their far-flung destinations. The Nile has the longest journey, for it re-emerges near Mount Atlas in west Africa. Almost immediately it disappears under the earth, finally reappearing and discharging into the Red Sea. The Ganges emerges at the foot of Mount Orcobares, and the Tigris and Euphrates at Mount Parachotra in Armenia. Maps usually showed the Four Rivers flowing out of Paradise, but found it impossible to show their subterranean courses. In honour of Paradise, the majority of medieval maps were oriented to the East and the Garden shown in a prominent position at the top of the map (see Figure 35).

Figure 31. The monstrous races one might expect to encounter on an Asian journey, from *Li Livres du Graunt Caam* (Marco Polo's *Travels*) by artist Johannes and his school. MS. Bodl. 264, fol. 260r (English, c. 1400).

The other map-shaping event from the Bible was the distribution of lands after the Flood to the sons of Noah. Although the Biblical account is far from clear, and many of the place-names are obscure, this transaction was interpreted in the Middle Ages to give Asia, the best and biggest continent with the most temperate climate, to Shem, as the oldest son. Ham got Africa, which was too hot for his taste and led him to invade Palestine, providing a peculiar justification for the Crusades many centuries later. Japhet, the youngest son, had to make do with chilly Europe (see Figure 34).

7

Medieval Islamic Geography

In the exuberant cultural flowering of Islamic society in the ninth century, most of the Greek scientific writings became available to Islamic scholars in their own tongue, but no Latin treatises. Whereas up to that time Greek ideas filtered down to the Latin West through the Roman and early Christian authors, the Islamic world received their Greek inheritance directly. The way in which the thought of earlier cultures reached medieval scholars is fundamental to understanding the manner in which ideas developed and the contrast between products of Islamic scholars and those of Christians of the same period. The lack of access to Latin materials, for example, suggests the reason why the T-O maps played no role in Islamic cartography.

Writing in about 150 AD, Ptolemy composed in Greek not only the astronomical treatise the *Almagest* already described but also a monumental *Geography*. Both were translated into Arabic in the early ninth century and stimulated an interest in geography and map-making. While the *Almagest* included a list of geographical coordinates for some places on the earth, his *Geography* provided coordinates for roughly 8,000 localities. In the *Almagest*, the ratio of the number of hours in the longest to those in the shortest day was used to establish latitude. In the *Geography* latitudes were determined from measurement of the height of the sun or pole star. Calculating longitude was trickier, but Ptolemy understood that the interval in longitude between two places could be found by establishing the local time of a lunar eclipse at both places. Unfortunately, not enough reliable data existed, and his figures, by his own admission, were necessarily approximate, based on travellers' estimates.

In the course of the *Geography*, Ptolemy discussed the requirements for making a map of the inhabited world. He, like all other scholars of his day, believed the earth to be spherical in form, with land masses

occupying about one-quarter of its surface and the rest covered by ocean. Anyone wishing to map the inhabited world is confronted by a problem: the surface of even one-quarter of a sphere cannot be represented on a flat map without distortion. Several methods of representing part of the surface of a sphere on a flat surface (called projections) were proposed by Greek scholars. Ptolemy singles out for criticism the one proposed by his near contemporary Marinus of Tyre, who in about 100 AD had suggested a rectangular grid (or graticule) of meridians and parallels on which latitudes and longitudes could be plotted. Ptolemy rejected Marinus' approach, except for use in regional maps, and proposed two mathematical projections of his own. Unfortunately, neither Marinus' nor Ptolemy's maps have been preserved, and it is uncertain whether Ptolemy ever actually made the maps which his *Geography* describes. The frequently reproduced 'world maps of Ptolemy' were constructed by European scholars in the early Renaissance following Ptolemy's text. It is curious that the Islamic world, which possessed the text of the *Geography* at an early date, made almost no direct use of it in map-making.

An important influence in the development of cartography in medieval Islam was the patronage of the caliph al-Ma'mūn, who ruled in Baghdad from 813 to 833. He commissioned several scholars to re-measure the distance on the surface of the earth that corresponded to one degree of celestial meridian. In this way he refined the definition of the mile (*mīl*) used by Arabs in comparison with the Greek unit of measure, the *stadion*, and also the calculation of the circumference of the earth. Another achievement of scholars working for al-Ma'mūn was the production of a large map of the world, unfortunately no longer preserved. What form the map of al-Ma'mūn took has prompted much speculation. Was it rectangular as Marinus proposed, or circular, or did it follow one of Ptolemy's non-rectilinear projections?

In the late tenth century, a Muslim geographer named Suhrāb accompanied a book of geographical coordinates with instructions for making a rectangular world map having horizontal and vertical scales for use in plotting the coordinates. The result of this procedure would have been (in modern terms) an equirectangular or cylindrical equidistant projection—essentially that proposed by Marinus of Tyre nine centuries earlier. Here again, no medieval examples of such a map exist today, though the carefully executed graphic scale on the rectangular map in the eleventh-century map in the *Book of Curiosities* (see Figure 39) suggests that such maps may have been in circulation.

There were several distinctive approaches to terrestrial mapping, one being that of the 'Balkhī school', so-called after its first proponent Abū Zayd al-Balkhī (d. 934), who was born in the city of Balkh in north-eastern Iran but spent most of his working life in Baghdad. The four geographers in this group, all working in the tenth century, wrote descriptions of the peoples, products, and customs of areas of the world then under Muslim domination; there was no interest in the non-Muslim world. No copies remain of al-Balkhī's treatise, but those of his three followers are preserved and each is accompanied by one world map and twenty-three regional maps, all closely related and characterized by a distinctive linear and abstract style (see Figures 38 & 42).

A second cartographic style can be seen in the anonymous *Book of Curiosities*. Compiled in Egypt between 1020 and 1050 (and copied about 150 years later), it contains a series of maps, both world and regional, many of which are without parallel. This recently discovered manuscript is a spectacular addition to our knowledge of medieval Islamic cosmography, geography, and map-making. The *Book of Curiosities* shows little influence from the 'Balkhī school', though it does appear that the author made use of other tenth-century maps. These maps are discussed in greater detail below.

In the early eleventh century, the versatile and highly creative scholar al-Bīrūnī produced a rather crude sketch map of land and water distribution that seems to have had a surprising amount of influence on later maps (Figure 32). The Nile is depicted as a broad channel dividing Africa in two, and it has been suggested that this map is the origin of the depiction of southern Africa as a forked peninsula that occurs in some later maps (for example, Figure 41). It is notable that Africa does not extend eastward towards China, in contrast to most world maps of this period where the African continent filled the southern hemisphere. That idea had been inherited from the astronomer and geographer Ptolemy but apparently was rejected by al-Bīrūnī for here Africa is so reduced that the Indian Ocean fills most of the southern hemisphere.

Probably the best-known medieval Islamic maps are those made by the Moroccan geographer al-Idrīsī about 1154 for Roger II, the Norman king of Sicily, to accompany his book for arm-chair travellers, *Entertainment for Him Who Longs to Travel the World*. At the core of his treatise is a set of seventy regional maps covering all the inhab-

Figure 32. Al-Bīrūnī's early 11th-
century sketch of land and water
distribution. MS Pococke 350, fol. 73b
(1539 [945H]).

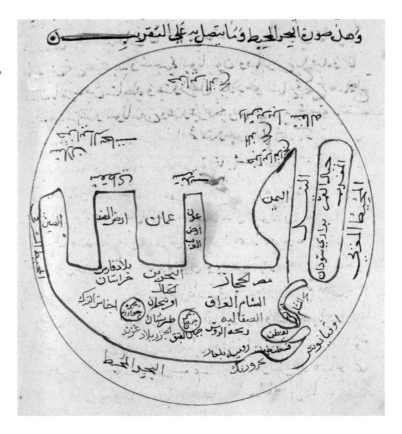

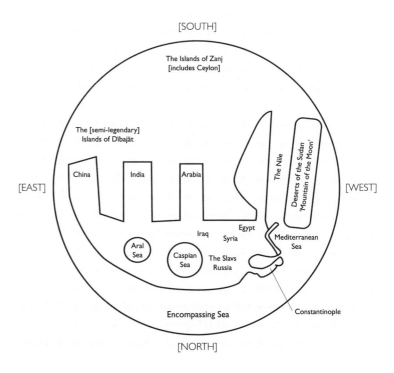

ited world. These included Christian territories, as was reasonable given that he was preparing it for a Christian ruler. Al-Idrīsī divided each of the seven classical 'climes', or latitudinal zones of the inhabited world as defined by Ptolemy, into ten subsections. As in the other map-making techniques described above, there is no reflection of the principles of projection and use of coordinates as advocated by Ptolemy. Ptolemy's influence is evident, however, in the reliance upon the system of astronomically defined 'climes' and the eastward extension of Africa.

The Islamic world also produced a unique style of map in diagrams for use in determining Qibla, the correct orientation toward Mecca. In the construction of mosques a niche facing Mecca must be placed accurately in the wall, so that those praying can orient themselves properly. The treatise on the determination of Qibla written in 1196 by the Egyptian legal scholar al-Dimyātī includes an example of a Qibla diagram (Figure 7), indicating the directions to be faced from four different localities (Aleppo, Damascus, Jerusalem, and Cairo) as well as pilgrimage routes, marked by squiggly lines. Similar diagrams often appear on astrolabes and other instruments known as Qibla-compasses.

Just as in Latin Europe, the Biblical 'Four Rivers of Paradise' played a role in Islamic cosmology, probably deriving from apocalyptic literature such as the *Book of the Secrets of Enoch*. The rivers were said to issue from a heavenly lotus-tree. Some said that the Nile and the Euphrates were two exterior rivers, while the other two were hidden Rivers of Paradise. Others identified the Four Rivers of Paradise with the earthly rivers of the Nile, the Euphrates, the Pyramus or Ceyhan river, which arises in eastern Turkey and flows into the Mediterranean, and the Saros or Syr Darya river, which arises near Tashkent in present-day Uzbekistan and flows into the Aral Sea. Yet others suggested these four rivers of the world were only counterparts to the paradisical rivers of honey, milk, wine, and water. In contrast to Western conventions, however, the Rivers of Paradise are never represented on Islamic maps nor do they seem to have had any influence on the cartographic tradition.

In addition to the Biblical Gog and Magog who dwelt in the far northeast, geographers loved to describe strange and monstrous races of people living at the edges of the inhabitable world. These curious creatures are never illustrated on any Islamic maps preserved today, in contrast to their frequent appearance on Western ones. Many of the

Figure 33. The Wāq-wāq tree from an Arabic miscellany compiled for the Mongol ruler of Baghdad, Sulṭān Aḥmad, who ruled 1382–1410. MS. Bodl. Or. 133, fol. 41b.

Figure 33a. The Wāq-wāq tree added by a later owner to the copy of the anonymous *Book of Curiosities* compiled about 1020–50. MS. Arab. c. 90, fol. 27a.

strange peoples are similar to those described in western writings (men with heads in the middle of their chest, for example), but one group, the Wāq-wāq, are unique to Islamic accounts. The explanation for their name was given by an anonymous twelfth-century Andalusian geographer as follows:[12]

> The island of Wāq-wāq is so called because of its great, tall trees there, with the many leaves like those of the fig-tree, except larger …In March, this tree sprouts fruit like those of the palm-tree but with the feet of young girls projecting from the base. On the second day of the month, two shins appear, and on the third day, two legs and two thighs. This continues, revealing a little more each day, until by the last day of April the whole torso has emerged. During May, the head appears, and the whole figure is complete, suspended by the hair. Their form and shape are most beautiful and desirable. At the beginning of June, they begin to drop from the trees and by the middle of the month not one remains. At the moment of falling, they utter two cries 'Wāq!-wāq!' … But once on the ground, they are found to be all flesh and no bones. Although they are more beautiful than words can describe, they have no life or soul. They are buried in the earth, for, were they to be left lying, no one would be able to approach them on account of the stench.

Just as the figures of Gog and Magog are not found on Islamic maps, though the barrier built by Alexander the Great to contain them is frequently depicted, so the labels 'Land of the Wāq-wāq' or 'Island of the Wāq-wāq' are found on medieval Islamic maps, but no drawings of the Wāq-wāq themselves. Illustrators of books on marvels, however, took all such strange creatures inhabiting inaccessible places as favourite subjects (Figure 33).

8

Mapping the Earth in the European Middle Ages

The concept of a spherical world was unambiguously transmitted from
classical antiquity to the Middle Ages. Most medieval writers simply
noted the fact, without the array of proofs which had been marshalled
by Aristotle in his treatise 'On the Heavens' (*De caelo*). Bede's evidence
was sensible though hardly derived from experience. According to
Bede, the stars visible to us in the northern hemisphere could not be
seen by the Troglodytes and Ethiopians in the southern hemisphere
due to the earth's sphericity; they have their own stars. The flat circular
disc of the T-O map was merely a convention, and some authors and
mapmakers, such as Matthew Paris, noted that the true shape of the
inhabited world was wider from east to west than it was from north to
south. There were probably some Flat-Earthers in medieval society,
but not among people with any claim to education. The conceit of the
medieval belief in a flat earth was invented in the nineteenth century,
in an attempt to promote the philosophy of progress. We are primarily
indebted to the American novelist Washington Irving for this misconception, for in his semi-historical *History of the Life and Voyages of
Christopher Columbus* published in 1828 he invented the idea that
Columbus was bravely defying the universally held notion that the
earth was flat.[13]

A world map in a computus or calendar manuscript at St John's
College, Oxford, completed in 1110, exhibits an unusual degree of
abstraction (Figure 34). It is circular, laid out like a T-O map, with
Asia at the top, and Europe occupying most of the lower (western)
section, while Africa is crowded into the lower right-hand corner. The
central bar of the map is not the Don-Nile north-south axis, but is
labelled 'Hierusalem', marked with a cross, the first example of Jerusalem clearly in the centre of a world map. Nearly all the places on the
map are closely connected to the Bible. Though Paradise itself is not

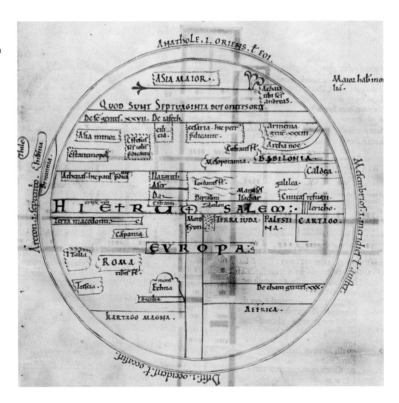

shown, we find the division of the earth among the sons of Noah, Noah's ark, seven of the twelve tribes of Israel, and Jericho. From the New Testament come the river Jordan, Galilee, and Nazareth, as well as Jerusalem. Athens, Ephesus, Achaia, and Caesarea are all places where the apostles preached. The manuscript is a lavish production made for the dedication of the church at the Benedictine monastery of Thorney in East Anglia, and contains numerous excerpts from astronomical and calendrical works for determining the dates of Easter and its attendant holidays. The map, with its peculiarly diagrammatic character, fits in well with the many other diagrams in the book.

By the thirteenth century a spectacular new version of the world map had developed in the Latin west, incorporating a full panoply of theological, historical, and philosophical characteristics. Smaller maps, preserved in books, could not display the full grandeur of the great *mappae mundi,* or maps of the world, such as the one from Hereford Cathedral, nearly five feet in diameter, but they were built on the same principles. The world map of Ranulf Higden of Chester (d. 1363) was made to illustrate his universal history *The Polychronicon,* and it does its best to give a full picture of the world in the small space of the manu-

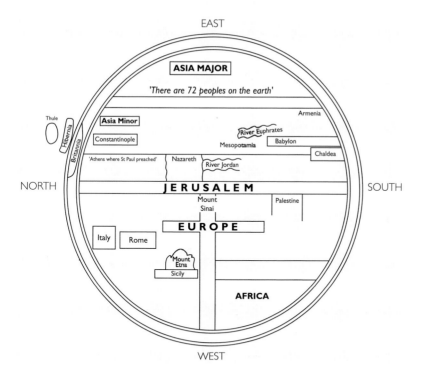

script page (see Figure 35). Oriented to the east, the location of the rising sun, it shows at the top a small scene of Adam and Eve in Paradise. Standing on either side of the Tree of Knowledge of Good and Evil, they are about to sample the fateful apple and be expelled from the 'Garden of Delights'. Perhaps Higden's book, packed with all sort of miscellaneous knowledge, could be thought of as a small compensation for the Fall.

Higden's map is oval rather than circular as most world maps of his day were, but this seems to have no special significance. The geographical shapes and province boundaries are schematic. Although much more realistic maps existed at the time, Higden chose not to use them and his map is deliberately archaic. The place-names are traditional, some dating back to the Roman Empire, such as the provincial names of Africa and Asia Minor, though this is an understandable practice in a work of history. Jerusalem, represented by a large, impressive castle, is in the centre of the map, as a statement of its spiritual importance. A number of place-names in Asia are taken from the Bible, such as the Jordan River, the city of Babylon, Galilee, and Mount Sinai. A path is drawn across the brightly-coloured Red Sea and labelled 'transitus

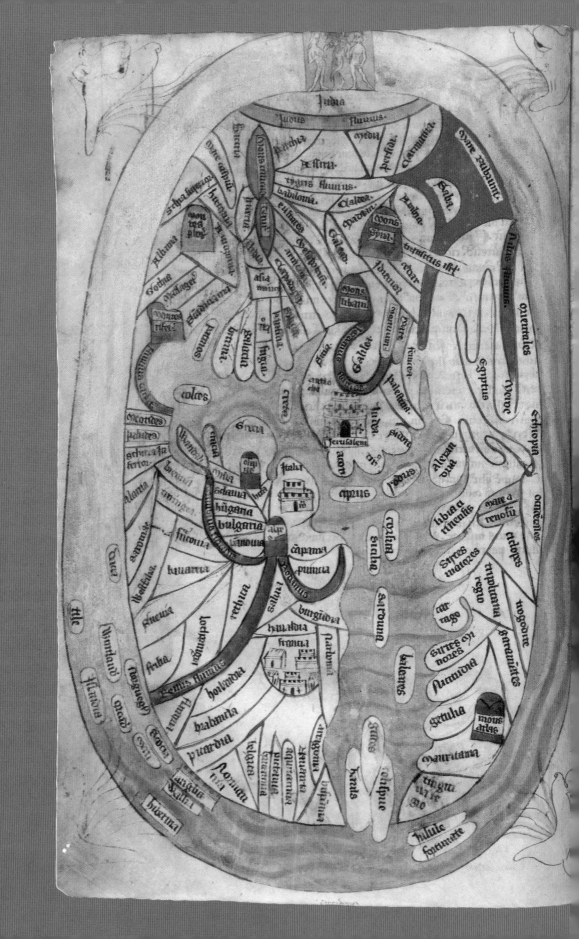

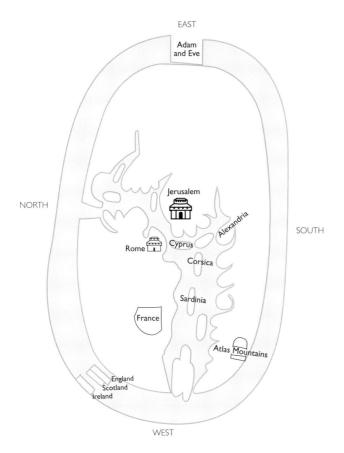

EAST

Adam
and Eve

Jerusalem

NORTH

Alexandria

SOUTH

Rome
Cyprus

Corsica

Sardinia

France

Atlas Mountains

England
Scotland
Ireland

WEST

Figure 35. World map from Ranulf Higden, *Polychronicon*, a universal history, showing Adam and Eve in Paradise at the top (east). MS. Tanner 170, fol. 15v

israel' for the passage of the Hebrews fleeing from the Pharaoh's oppressive rule. The many points of interest in the Holy Land led some mapmakers to enlarge it in relation to the rest of the world, in order to fit everything in.

Other standard geographical features in Higden's map include the River Nile, shown wandering all over Africa before emptying into the Mediterranean Sea near the city of Alexandria, and the island of Gades (Cadiz) labelled with the columns of Hercules, here written out in words, but sometimes shown as columns. These indicated the end of the Mediterranean, and, traditionally, the limits of (sane) human travel. The world is surrounded by a narrow band of Ocean in which a number of islands can be found, including the British Isles, Norway, and the more problematic islands of Wintlandia, Tile, and the Fortunate Islands. On a Higden map now in the British Library, the edges of the world are crowded with inscriptions describing the various monstrous races and exotic animals to be found in those regions, all taken from Higden's text. The only monsters on this map are the four wind

Figure 36. World map drawn by
Pietro Vesconte for Marino Sanudo,
1321, integrating the techniques and
forms of the sea chart with a map of
the world with East at the top. MS.
Tanner 190, fols. 203v–204r.

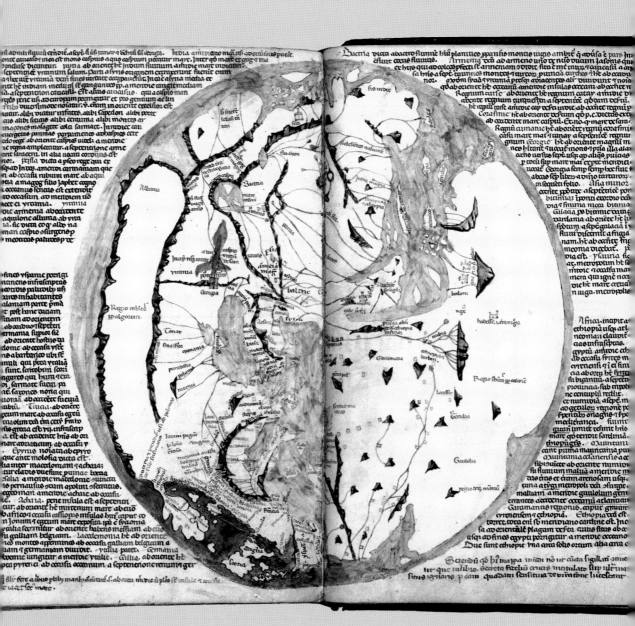

monsters which blow from outside its limits. Not all of his place-names are antique, for in Europe he includes Holland, Hungary, Brabant and Flanders, as well as Thuringia, Westphalia, and Aragon. France is marked by a group of buildings, possibly meant for Paris.

Maps were made to illustrate numerous copies of Higden's work, some less beautifully coloured than this one and some merely arranged as list-maps without any geographical features. Higden's book, which opens with a lengthy set of chapters on world geography, expands upon the map in greater detail, adding historical anecdotes and moral lessons to the mere recitation of place-names.

Working in the same century as Higden, another map maker created a very different map at the behest of Marino Sanudo, a citizen of Venice campaigning for a revival of the Crusades (see Figure 36). The fall of the city of Acre to the Saracens in 1291 had left the Europeans without a foothold on the mainland, banishing them to the island of Cyprus. Sanudo, a member of a wealthy mercantile family with possessions in the Aegean islands, had pursued an energetic career in business before turning to his mission as a promoter of the reconquest of the Holy Land. His book, entitled *Book of Secrets for True Crusaders,* included Biblical history, the history of the Crusades, the geography of the Holy Land, and practical strategies for reclaiming it for the West. He proudly presented a copy to the Pope in 1321. The book was copiously illuminated not only with miniatures (for example, Figure 37), but also with a set of maps, made by one of the first professional mapmakers, Pietro Vesconte of Genoa. Vesconte was a maker of nautical charts, and the results of his experience can be seen clearly in the world and regional maps he made for Sanudo. In the areas of the Mediterranean and Black Seas and the Atlantic coast the geographical forms are precise, reflecting a mariner's reality, rather than the abstract shapes which sufficed to make up Higden's world.

Strikingly, Sanudo's world map as drawn by Vesconte (Figure 36) contains no overt religious content. Paradise is not shown, nor are there angels flanking the map nor Christ sitting in judgment above. It was not that Sanudo was not religious; he was a devout, not to say fanatical, Christian. When it came to maps, however, as when it came to finances, this hard-headed Venetian businessman was determined to make no mistakes. He was convinced that woolly-headedness had been responsible for the failure of previous Crusades and he wanted his to be administered in a more realistic spirit.

The Vesconte map shows some interesting developments in its geographical forms. Beyond the accuracy of the frequently travelled seas, the shape of Africa has altered. It extends to the east, where it is separated from Asia, not by the Nile, but by an Indian Ocean which is open on its eastern end—typical of Islamic maps. In the Indian Ocean and in Asia we see new details which may have come from medieval travellers in this area in the thirteenth century, such as Marco Polo, another Venetian. One of the new features is a landlocked Caspian Sea. The position of the Caspian had been known to Ptolemy, but that information had not been handed down to the West, for medieval maps usually showed the Caspian as a gulf of the northern ocean. By the end of the thirteenth century, however, news of the true site of the Caspian began to come back in travel accounts. Also in Asia Vesconte notes the presence of the Tartars, who had recently forced themselves on European attention, as well as the territory of the 'Great Khan' and his kingdom of Cathay.

9

Medieval Islamic Mapping of the World

Unlike medieval European map makers, Islamic cartographers inherited the geographical writings of Ptolemy and the cosmological writings of Aristotle. On the other hand, the early Latin geographical tradition, including Pliny and Macrobius, were unknown to Arabic scholars. Surviving Islamic maps clearly reveal several traditions of map making, perhaps the most distinctive of which is the so-called Balkhī school mentioned earlier. Stylised line-work and extreme abstraction of geographic forms characterize the products of this group of tenth-century geographers working in or near Baghdad. The world map shown in Figure 38 was drawn in 1297 by the Persian translator of the *Book of Routes and Provinces* by al-Iṣṭakhrī (d. *c.*951) of the 'Balkhī school'. South is at the top and the inhabited world is a circle surrounded by the broad band of the Encompassing Sea. There is an eastward extension of Africa so that nearly the entire southern (top) quadrant is land. Two seas (with nearly parallel shores) approach the centre: the Indian Ocean from the east and the Mediterranean from the west. The River Nile arises in Africa and flows through a straight channel northward (downward) into the Mediterranean.

Another tradition of world maps, the rectangular world map in the *Book of Curiosities* is entirely different and until recently completely unknown (Figure 39). At the top a carefully executed graphic scale is strikingly suggestive of a method for plotting a world map proposed in the late tenth century by the Muslim geographer Suhrāb. Nonetheless, the map as we have it today has not been mathematically plotted, though it may be a poor copy or sketch, many times removed, of a more carefully constructed original. The map does not, in fact, represent the whole of the inhabited world for much of northern Europe and Asia are not depicted.

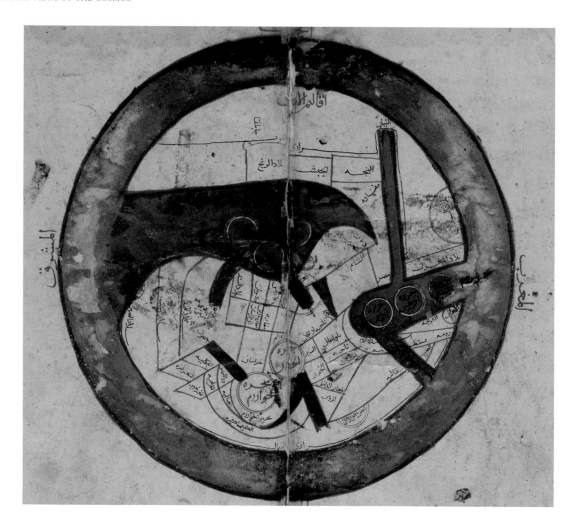

Figure 38. World map by the 'Balkhī School' from a Persian translation of *Kitāb al-Masālik wa-al-mamālik* ('Book of Routes and Provinces') by al-Iṣṭakhrī (d. c. 951). MS. Ouseley 373, fols. 3b–4a (1297 [696 H]).

The 'Mountain of the Moon', thought to be the source of the River Nile, has been painted over the centre of the scale. Europe is depicted as a landmass to the lower right, with a very large Iberian peninsula. No islands are shown in the Mediterranean, perhaps because other maps in the treatise are devoted solely to the Mediterranean and to the islands of Sicily and Cyprus. At the left-hand margin of the map, a brown landmass has an inscription reading: 'Island of the Jewel, and its mountains encircle it like a basket'— this island, usually interpreted as Indonesia or Formosa, was considered the easternmost limit of the inhabitable world. The map also depicts, in the lower left corner, the legendary wall constructed by Alexander the Great to imprison Gog and Magog. At the Caspian Sea, represented by a dark circle in the lower left quadrant, a number of tributaries converge, one of which flows from Gog and Magog's

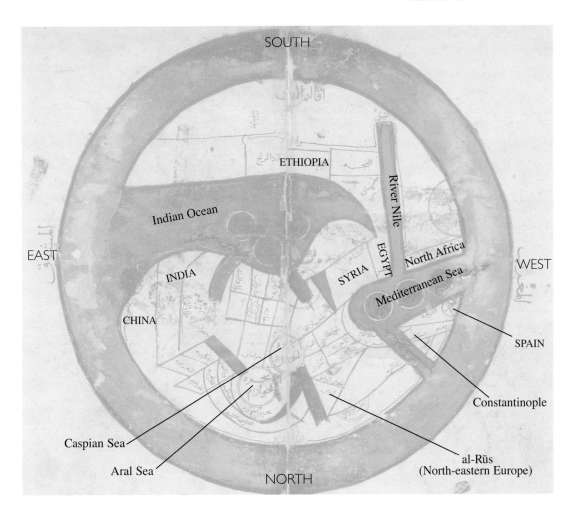

SOUTH

ETHIOPIA

River Nile

Indian Ocean

EAST

WEST

INDIA

EGYPT

SYRIA

North Africa

Mediterranean Sea

SPAIN

CHINA

Constantinople

Caspian Sea

Aral Sea

al-Rūs
(North-eastern Europe)

NORTH

mountain enclave. Unlike European map makers, the Islamic cartographers always showed the Caspian as an inland sea.

The author's interest in travel and trade is evident in the several routes or itineraries that he placed somewhat arbitrarily on top of the map. In Spain, for example, the long straight line of red dots is an itinerary beginning near Toledo and proceeding through Lisbon to Cordoba and on to Almería on the southern coast. Itineraries are given from Kufa (south of Karbala in Iraq) to Damascus and, in the other direction, from Kufa to Mecca. The Tunisian coast has been exaggerated in length in order to accommodate another itinerary.

The third approach to world maps is exemplified by the well-known circular world map of al-Idrīsī associated with his geographic

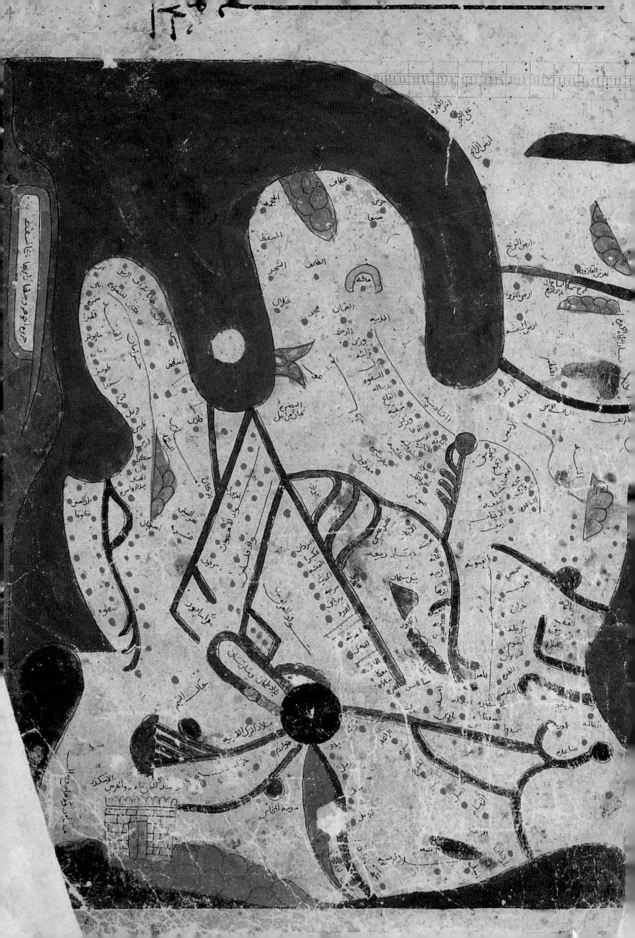

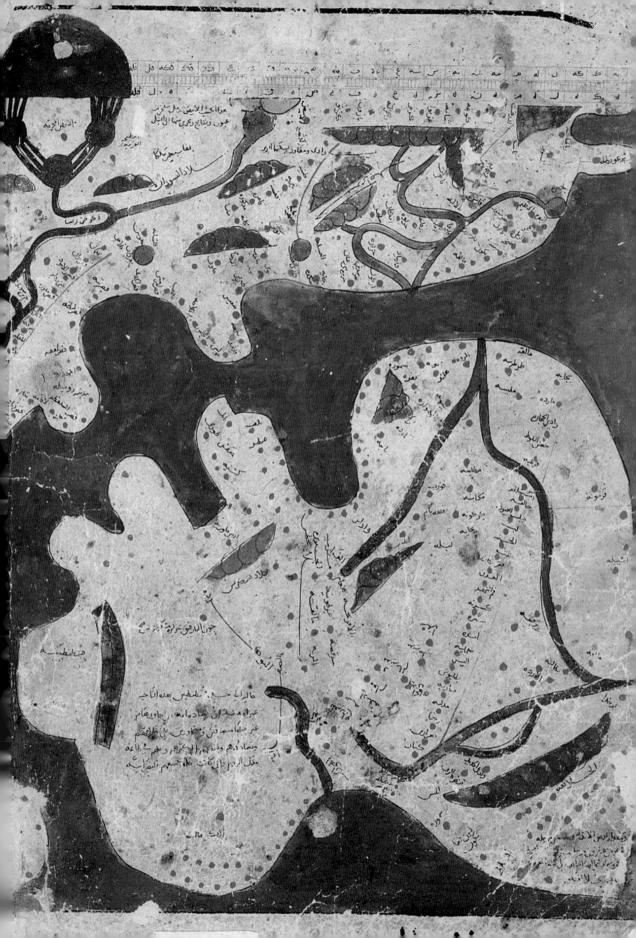

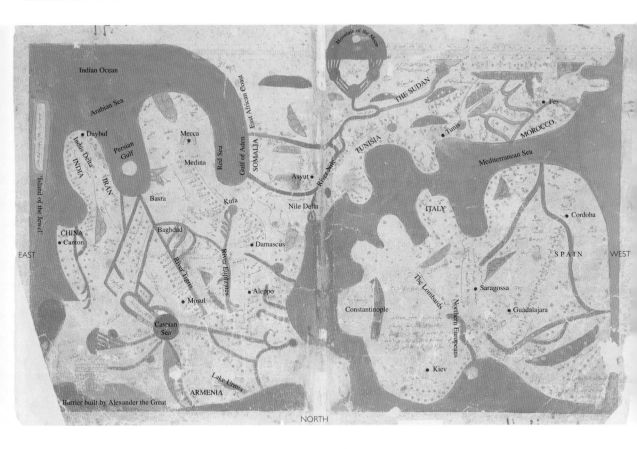

The labels visible on the map include:

Mountain of the Moon · Indian Ocean · THE SUDAN · Fes · Arabian Sea · East African Coast · MOROCCO · Daybul · Mecca · Tunis · TUNISIA · Persian Gulf · Medina · Red Sea · Gulf of Aden · SOMALIA · Mediterranean Sea · Indus Delta · INDIA · IRAN · Basra · Kufa · Asyut · River Nile · Nile Delta · ITALY · Cordoba · 'Island of the Jewel' · CHINA · Baghdad · Damascus · SPAIN · Canton · EAST · River Tigris · River Euphrates · The Lombards · Saragossa · WEST · Aleppo · Constantinople · Guadalajara · Mosul · Northern Europeans · Caspian Sea · Kiev · Lake Urmia · ARMENIA · Barrier built by Alexander the Great · NORTH

compendium made in 1154 for Roger II of Sicily. The circular world map found in the *Book of Curiosities* (Figure 40) is virtually identical but produced a full century earlier. It illustrates the inhabited world surrounded by a dark ring representing the 'Encompassing Sea'. South is at the top, with the African land mass extending eastward so that it covers virtually all the southern hemisphere. Seven concentric arcs indicate the seven classical 'climes', the uppermost arc representing the equator. The Indian Ocean is land-locked except for a narrow opening due east, and along its upper (southern) shore four small umbrella-like structures represent mountains from which rivers rise and empty into the Indian Ocean. To the east is the land of the Wāq-wāq, and at the lower left can be seen Gog and Magog's wall. The Caspian Sea is an elongated oval near the centre of the map. At the lower right of the map (which has been damaged) England is shown as a small oval island labelled in Arabic *Inqiltarah* (or *Inghiltirah*) —that is, Angle-Terre— possibly the earliest depiction of Britain with such a designation.

If, as present evidence suggests, *The Book of Curiosities* was composed in 1020–1050, then the world map generally known as 'al-Idrīsī's map'

did not originate with him, but was designed well before his birth. It is possible that copyists have simply inserted this earlier map into copies of al-Idrīsī's treatise, since al-Idrīsī himself does not refer to such a world map in the text, but only to his 70 regional maps.

A blend of cartographic traditions is evident in an anonymous Arabic treatise titled *The Book of Creation and History* produced in North Africa in 1570 (Figure 41). The map is oriented with East, not south, at the top. Its features are a composite of several traditions: The open Indian Ocean and the forked south African coast reflect al-Bīrūnī's eleventh-century sketch of landmasses (see Figure 32). The general form of the northern hemisphere, the seven concentric arcs representing the seven 'climes', the barrier against Gog and Magog, and the small square island labelled *Inghiltrah* (Angle-Terre or England) are all reminiscent of the circular world map in the *Book of Curiosities* and associated with al-Idrīsī (see Figure 40).

Some of the features evident in these Islamic maps, such as the shape of the Indian Ocean, the eastward extension of Africa, the enclosed Caspian Sea, and place-names in Asia and Africa, can also be seen in the map drawn in 1321 by Pietro Vesconte (see Figure 36). They strongly suggest that an Islamic map was available in Italy by the early fourteenth century, possibly obtained by Sanudo on his extensive travels in the East. A number of the fifteenth-century European maps, such as the great world map of Fra Mauro in Venice, were drawn with south on top, Arab-style. On the other hand, the Arabic map produced in 1570 in North Africa (Figure 41) suggests some European influence, for example in its eastern orientation. It is quite likely that there was more frequent interchange of intellectual commodities between the northern and southern rims of the Mediterranean than has been generally supposed.

Figure 40. The circular world map from the *Book of Curiosities* compiled about 1020–1050. MS. Arab. c. 90, fols. 27b–28a (12th–13th century).

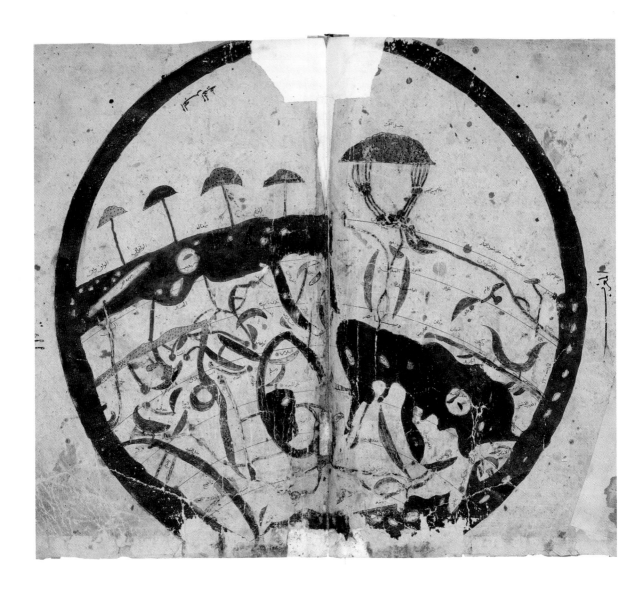

SOUTH

Mountain of the Moon

Land of the Waq-Waq

Land of the Waq-Waq

MOZAMBIQUE

ETHIOPIA

River Nile

CEYLON

Indian Ocean

OMAN

JAVA

EAST

WEST

INDIA

Persian Gulf

CHINA

EGYPT

TIBET

CYPRUS

CRETE

Mediterranean Sea

Atlas Mountains

SICILY

TUNISIA

MOROCCO

Caspian Sea

ITALY

SPAIN

Barrier built by Alexander the Great

MACEDONIA

Gog

The Alps

BRITTANY

Magog

POLAND

ENGLAND

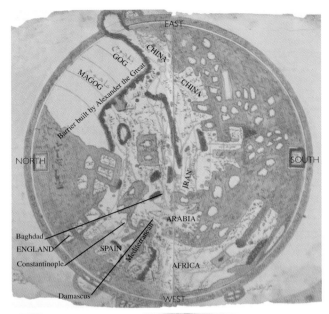

Figure 41. A world map from an anonymous Arabic treatise titled *Book of Creation and History* (*Kitāb al-Bad' wa-al-ta'rīkh*) produced in North Africa in 1570. MS. Laud Or. 317, fol. 10b–11a.

10

Medieval Islamic Regional Mapping

As with world maps, Islamic regional maps can also be grouped into
three basic types. The earliest is that associated with the tenth-century
'Balkhī school'. These maps covered the Islamic empire only and not
any non-Muslim territories. The boundaries were political ones, not
astronomically defined 'climes'. The example shown here (Figure 42) is
a map of Syria made by al-Iṣṭakhrī (d. c.951). The distances between
stops, indicated by circles or polygonal shapes, were equalized. Only
verticals, horizontals, 90-degree angles, and arcs of circles were employed in the design, and all surface geographical detail has been
eliminated except for a toothed band representing a mountain range.
The same principles were employed in 1931 by Harry Beck when he
designed the *London Underground Map*—an approach particularly useful
for memory and organization of routes. And routes or itineraries were
at the heart of the treatises by the so-called 'Balkhī school' that these
'maps' accompanied.

The second approach is that devised by al-Idrīsī for his treatise on
geography compiled in Palermo in 1154. Al-Idrīsī considered the
extent of the habitable world to be 160° in longitude. For latitiude, he
followed the system of seven 'climes' defined astronomically by the
length of the longest day of the year in each of the seven regions,
dividing each of the seven bands into ten sections, each 16° wide. The
result was seventy regional maps covering the inhabited world. It was
an ingenious system, and the copies that we have are a feast for the
eyes. The sectional map shown here (Figure 43) covers the area of the
Mediterranean Sea around Sicily. South is at the top. The island has its
characteristic triangular shape and is set in the midst of its archipelago
with the toe of Calabria to the left and Sardinia to the right. The
principal rivers and dominant relief are indicated in stylised but
recognisable form.

Figure 42. A map of Syria (with South at the top) by the 'Balkhī school', from a Persian translation of *Kitāb al-Masālik wa-al-mamālik* ('Book of Routes and Provinces') by al-Iṣṭakhrī (d. c.951). MS. Ouseley 373, fol. 33b (1297 [696H]).

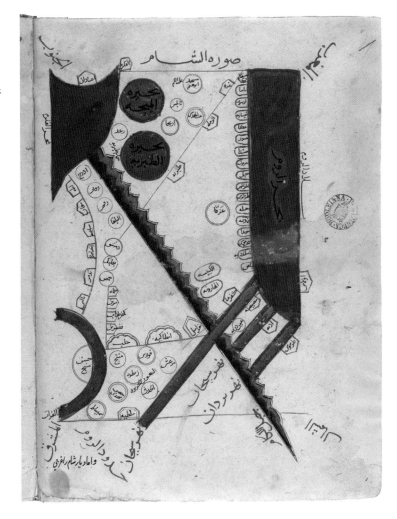

A different approach to map-making is found in the twelve regional maps in the *Book of Curiosities*. The map of the island of Sicily (Figure 44) is conceived very differently from that by al-Idrīsī and provides important new information through its numerous labels and accompanying text about the island in the period just before the Norman invasion. North is at the top of this map. Unlike al-Idrīsī's later map of the island, the map in the *Book of Curiosities* was apparently based on a written list or itinerary. That itinerary must have been incomplete, however, because approximately one third of the coastal periphery is omitted. This error accounts for the most conspicuous anomaly of the map—the appearance of Mount Etna, with its crown of fire, not in the north-east but in the south-west of the island. The walled city of Palermo, with its gates and port guarded by two towers, dominates the map. The hinterland of Palermo, with its suburbs, streams and copious

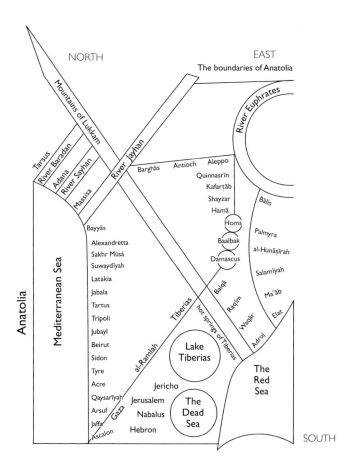

NORTH

EAST

The boundaries of Anatolia

River Euphrates

Mountains of Lukkam

Tarsus

River Baradan

Adana

River Sayhan

River Jayhan

Barghās Antioch Aleppo

Massisa

Quinnasrīn

Kafartāb

Shayzar

Bālis

Ḥamā

Bayyās

Homs

Palmyra

Alexandretta

Baalbak

al-Ḥunāṣīrah

Sakhr Mūsá

Damascus

Suwaydīyah

Salamīyah

Latakia

Jabala

Balqā

Maʿāb

Tartus

Raqim

Tiberias

Tripoli

Waqār

hot springs of Tiberias

Elat

Jubayl

Beirut

Adruḥ

Mediterranean Sea

Anatolia

al-Ramlah

Sidon

Lake
Tiberias

Tyre

The
Red
Sea

Acre

Jericho

Qaysarīyah

Jerusalem

Gaza

The
Dead
Sea

Arsuf

Nabalus

Jaffa

Hebron

Ascalon

SOUTH

Diagram of map of Syria, inverted
with North at the top.

springs, is shown as stretching almost to the opposite coast of the
island—a fantastic perspective which emphasizes the extent to which,
for a contemporary observer, Palermo *was* Sicily.

The unknown author of the *Book of Curiosities* was especially
knowledgeable about the eastern Mediterranean. In addition to the
map of Sicily, there is a diagrammatic map of Cyprus—the earliest
known—that is in effect a written text providing detailed information
about its twenty-seven harbours, indicating the island's importance as
an emporium for trade between Byzantium and the Islamic
Mediterranean.

There are also two maps of coastal cities: the Tunisian city of al-
Mahdīyah and the commercial centre in the Nile Delta, Tinnīs. The
author of the *Book of Curiosities* evidently recognised the authority of

the Fāṭimid imāms who came to power in Ifrīqiyah (modern Tunisia) in 909 and ruled in Cairo from 973 until the dynasty was overthrown in 1171. His allegiance to the Fāṭimids may explain why he provides the earliest map of al-Mahdīyah, founded in 921 as their first capital (Figure 45), and at that time one of the most important centres of Mediterranean trade. The peninsular city is shown surrounded by stone walls, and is depicted in bird's-eye view, as if seen from the south-west. The four cardinal directions are indicated around the map with east at the top. The city's fortified port, surrounded by harbour buildings, is depicted in the upper right corner. The two isolated and rather elaborate buildings are labelled prominently: 'the palaces of the [Fāṭimid] imams, may peace be upon them'. In the top left quadrant is an itinerary of the route from al-Mahdīyah to Palermo.

The map of Tinnīs is a unique record, depicting this town evacuated in 1189 and then totally destroyed by the Crusaders in 1227. In the early eleventh century, however, Tinnīs was a great commercial city, one of the principal centres for the production and trade of textiles. The city, built on an island in the Nile Delta, is represented as a rectangle, bounded by massive walls, with the Mediterranean at the top and the deltaic lake on the other three sides. The simplified diagram provides a platform for a written description of the city. Only two features are represented pictorially: the rectangular enclosure of its walls and two channels labelled 'the inlets for the waters', which illustrate a phenomenon described in the text. Every year, after the salt waters of the lake were driven out to sea by the sweet waters of the flooding Nile, these channels were opened to allow the floodwater to refill the huge cisterns upon which the city depended for its water supply. So much attention is given Tinnīs in the *Book of Curiosities* that it is tempting to think the author was a native of that city and perhaps himself involved in its commerce.

The *Book of Curiosities* also has a unique map of the Mediterranean Sea as a whole (Figure 46). The dark green sea, oval in form, is crammed with 120 islands, with Sicily and Cyprus shown as rectangles. Around the periphery, 121 anchorages on the mainland are described, with information on winds and landmarks, suggesting an itinerary along the eastern Mediterranean. The straits of Gibraltar are indicated by thin red lines at the far left of the oval. The utilitarian nature of this 'map' may be responsible for its concentration on the Byzantine and Islamic shores of the Mediterranean at the expense of the Christian West, and Islamic Spain, which are all but ignored.

Figure 43. The map of Sicily from the
*Entertainment for He Who Longs to
Travel the World* (*Nuzhat al-mushtāq fī
ikhtirāq al-āfāq*), compiled about 1154
by the Moroccan scholar al-Idrīsī.
MS. Pococke 375, fols. 187b–188a
(1553 [960H]).

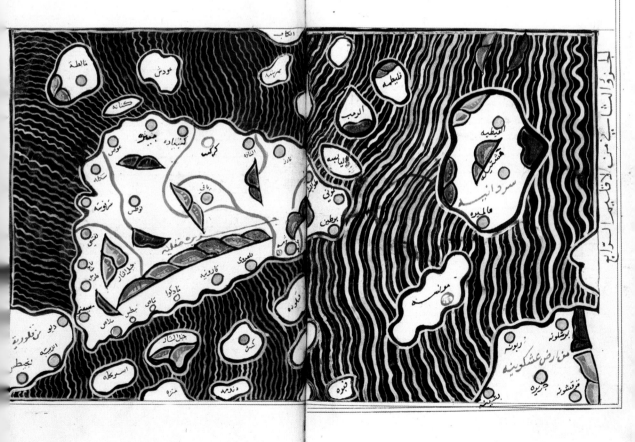

Figure 44. The island of Sicily from the *Book of Curiosities* compiled about 1020–1050. MS. Arab. c. 90, fols. 32b–33a (12th–13th century).

Figure 45. The Tunisian city of al-Mahdiyah from the *Book of Curiosities* compiled about 1020–1050. MS. Arab. c. 90, folio 34a (12th–13th century)

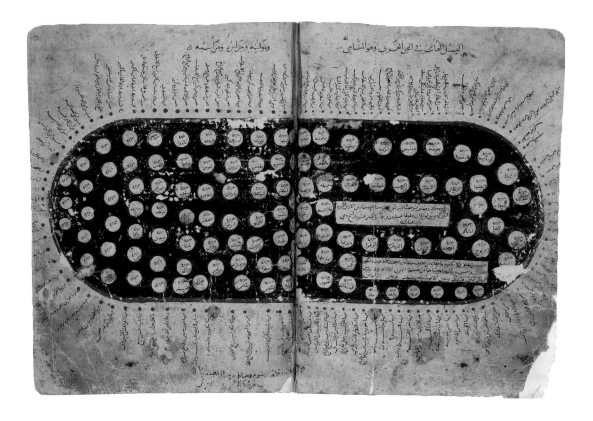

Interest in the eastern Mediterranean is further illustrated by a diagram of the 'Bays of Byzantium', which opens a navigational guide to twenty-eight ports of the Aegean Sea. This guide to the Aegean begins very near the bay on the Turkish coast (opposite the island of Rhodes) where in the 1970s a ship-wreck was discovered dating to about 1025, the time of the composition of the *Book of Curiosities*. The ship came from Egypt, as did almost certainly the author of the *Book of Curiosities*. This recently discovered manuscript corroborates information gained from the shipwreck and provides new information on the patterns of Arab trade in the waters of the eastern Mediterranean, for the most part under Byzantine control in the early eleventh century.

The Mediterranean, however, was not the only concern of the author of the *Book of Curiosities*. His map of the Indian Ocean (Figure 47) is also oval in shape and combines the Indian Ocean with the South China Sea, the Bay of Bengal, the Arabian Sea, the Gulf of Aden, and the waters off the east coast of Africa. It is possible that the author was

Figure 46 *above*. The Mediterranean Sea from the *Book of Curiosities* compiled about 1020–1050. MS. Arab. c. 90, fols 31b–32a (12th–13th cent.).

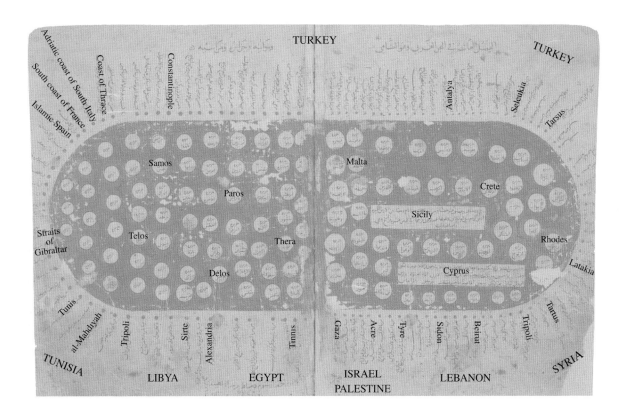

following Ptolemy in representing the Indian Ocean as an enclosed sea, though it may be that he simply found the oval format useful for displaying information, particularly itineraries, as he had done with the Mediterranean. The map is in two distinct parts: on the right, the eastern half of the Indian Ocean with Indian and Chinese localities represented along its shores; on the left, the east African coasts and islands. The large island with red dots at the centre of the map (mostly lost in the gutter of the manuscript) is probably Ceylon. In the present copy the two eastern and western halves of the map have been wrongly sited, possibly as a result of a copying technique producing a mirror image. Instead of connecting China with Africa, the right and left halves of the map are joined so that China links up with the Arabian Peninsula, while the east African coast and the coasts of India appear to form one land mass. Moreover, some of the itineraries within each section of the map have been written down in an inverse order, making this copy of the map very impractical to use.

The combining of distinct entities into one schematic feature is also evident in the *Book of Curiosities*'s five maps of the river systems (the rivers Nile, Oxus, Euphrates, Tigris, and Indus). For example, the map of the Indus (Figure 48) represents the three major rivers of northern India—the Indus, Ganges, and Brahmaputra—as a single river system that has its origins in the mountains of Tibet, runs from east to west and eventually flows into the Indian Ocean. In reality, the Indus runs westwards from the Himalayas, while the Ganges and the Brahmaputra flow into the Bay of Bengal, though the sources of these rivers were still being explored in the nineteenth century. Two itineraries are displayed on the map: one from the Islamic capital in India, al-Multān, to the Hindu capital of Qanawj on the banks of the Ganges, and the second from Qanawj on to China. These suggest that commercial routes crossed political boundaries between the Islamic and Hindu states of northern India, and that Muslim traders in the early eleventh century knew, and possibly used, the overland route between India and China.

Figure 47 *above*. The Indian Ocean from the *Book of Curiosities* compiled about 1020–1050. MS. Arab. c. 90, fols. 29b–30a (12th–13th century).

Such river diagrams are without parallel in the preserved literature, except for the drawing of the River Nile (Figure 49). This page in the *Book of Curiosities* has been damaged, so that only the 'Mountain of the

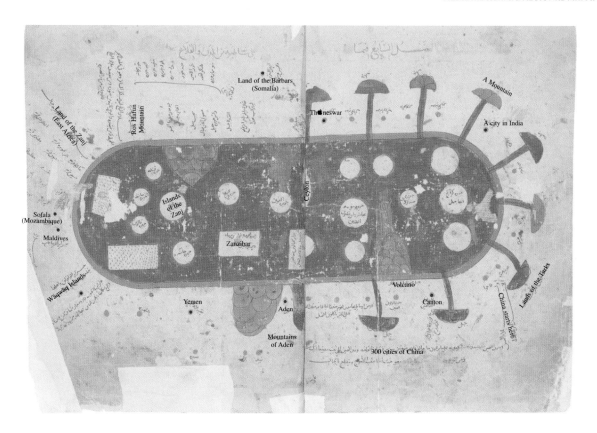

Moon' is visible. Accounts of the snow-clad summit of Kilimanjaro
may have prompted this ancient conception of the source for the Nile,
also referred to by Ptolemy in the plural 'Mountains of the Moon'.
Beneath (that is, north of) the Mountain of the Moon are three
marshes into which the waters flow through several tributaries before
joining with a large tributary from the west to form the main channel
of the river. This schematic conception of the origins of the Nile,
which was an elaboration of classical descriptions of the river, is
strikingly similar to the map of the Nile by al-Khwārazmī (d. c.847).
Only fragments have survived of the maps made by the mathematician,
astronomer, and geographer al-Khwārazmī, the earliest extant Islamic
maps, and it is likely that his work served as the source for several other
maps found in the *Book of Curiosities*. The origin of the Nile was a
topic of major interest to geographers since classical times, though its
true source was not discovered until the nineteenth century. Similar
Nile diagrams are found in later Arabic treatises, often incorporated
into world maps. Since Islamic world maps are generally orientated
with south at the top, the Mountain of the Moon is easily identifiable
as the uppermost object on the map, marking the southern limit of the
habitable world (see for example Figures 39, & 40).

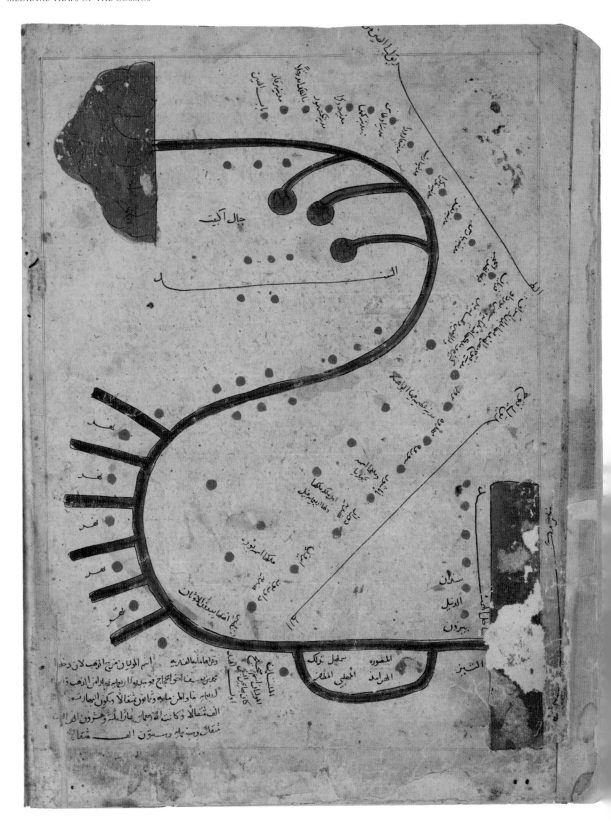

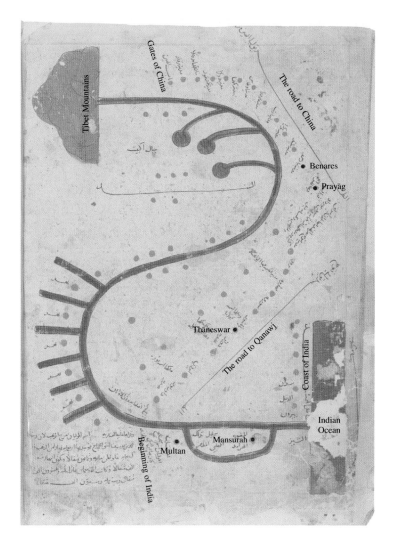

Figure 48. The Indus River from the *Book of Curiosities* compiled about 1020–1050. MS. Arab. c. 90, fol. 43b (12th–13th century).

Figure 49 *following page*. The River Nile from the *Book of Curiosities* compiled about 1020–1050. MS. Arab c. 90, fol. 42a (12th–13th century).

11

Regional Mapping in Medieval Europe

Regional and local maps that have survived from the European Middle
Ages are far fewer than world maps from the same period. World
maps, usually included as illustrations in scientific and philosophical
books, tended to be preserved more often than maps of less sweeping
scope. We find a scattering of regional maps, from Gerald of Wales'
map of the British Isles (*c.*1200) to a number of maps of the Holy Land.
One of the most interesting medieval regional maps was originally in a
Bible at Corpus Christi College, Oxford (Figure 50). It was preserved
not for its own sake but for the painting of the three Maries at the
tomb of Christ, which is on the other side. The Bible was copied in
part by Matthew Paris, and his hand has also been identified on the
map. Employed as the chronicler for St Alban's Abbey 1235–59,
Matthew was the author of the *Chronica Majora*, an important record of
national and international affairs as well as matters of more local
interest. One of the issues which perpetually surfaced was that of the
Crusades. One such venture, headed up by Richard of Cornwall,
brother of the king of England, was several years getting going, from
1236, when he took the cross, until 1240, when he actually set sail.
Matthew's interest in the Crusade can be seen in the map he drew,
which may have been made as a set of pictorial notes for his chronicle.
The map (Figure 50) is relatively plain and unadorned. North, with the
land of Antioch and the mountain stronghold of the assassins, is at the
top, and the cities of the coast are ranged down the left-hand side. To
the east are Damascus, the Sea of Galilee, and the Dead Sea. In addition to place-names of cities, castles, monasteries, and important
religious sites, Matthew includes estimated distances in terms of days'
journeys. On the side of the page he has written several notes to
himself, correcting errors (the river Jordan does not flow through
Damascus as shown) and adding more information (it is 300 leagues
from Acre to Cyprus). Matthew's map is a working document, in-

Figure 50 *right*. An unusually factual map of the Holy Land by Matthew Paris, England's most creative 13th-century cartographer. North is at the top, coastal cities at the left, and Egypt below. Oxford, Corpus Christi College, MS 2* (English, mid-13th century).

tended for use and not for show. He made several other maps of the Holy Land, which were bound with his chronicles, and these are more ornamental, with fewer place-names and more pictures. We know of no antecedent to this map. Perhaps there was none; Matthew Paris was an unusually creative and original thinker and was completely capable of producing this map himself, compiling it from information that came to him at his post at the Abbey.

World maps of this period often included an expanded space for the Holy Land. The world map (Figure 36) made by Vesconte in 1321 for Marino Sanudo had room for only a few names in the Holy Land, without distorting the scale, and so a whole separate map of this region was drawn (Figure 51). This map is notable for its grid covering the entire map, with each square equalling two leagues. It is one of the first maps in the West to be drawn to scale, although it is not entirely accurate. Holy places are duly included, but the primary purpose of the map is to give a clear picture of the Crusades' military objective. To the invader it is necessary to know exactly how far apart places are.

Sanudo included other maps in his book, all probably drawn by Vesconte: a sea chart of the eastern Mediterranean and city plans for Jerusalem and the important port city of Acre (see Figures 52 & 53). Some editions of the book also have additional sea charts, covering the rest of the Mediterranean. The text itself contains a written portolan, or set of sailing directions, for the eastern Mediterranean coasts. Vesconte's map-making, and Sanudo's use of it, shows a concept of the map which was different from that of the encyclopaedic *mappa mundi*. Running parallel with the monumental map tradition was a functional approach to mapping, seen most importantly in the work of those who made and used the sea charts. To the mariner, reaching one's destination without running aground was more important than seeing the world in its full historical and theological significance. Or perhaps it would be more true to say that both were important. The Venetian galley captain, Andrea Bianco, included a *mappa mundi* as part of his 1436 atlas of sea charts.

The marine charts, which first appear in Europe in the late thirteenth century, are quite different from any other medieval maps. Showing the frequently travelled coasts of the Mediterranean and Black Seas and the Atlantic, the maps are amazingly similar in form to those with which we are familiar today. The example shown in Figure 54 is one of seven fifteenth-century Spanish sea charts that form a set bound in

Terra ... damasci

mons libani ...
habitacio Assessinorum

castrum hospitalis
Crac ...
castrum dni de ... mon.

Abbacia
Eva ca me li.

Terra Palestina ... inhabitabilis ... dns soldan' damasci.

cedri z ebeni

mons libanus ...
font Ior ...

flum̄ Damasci

Tur ... R ... R ... G ... R

... flum̄ ...
Damasci

Recordane.

Scm̄ georgē

Iste ... Iudee Syria ... Palestina ... ista

Sefrem
planicies sabe

Nazareth
cas' ...

cas' Safauie

cas' Cana galilee

Tena ista est ...

planicies et sabe
habitacio laban.

Nazareth
... galilee
mons tabor

cas' Cacho

cas' Capol ...
mons ... mon.
Saga dni

Sichar
mons
Gelboe

caimis
Sebaste

Ramatha
Bethnople

Scus Samuel

civitas ...

civitas Sion

IERUSALEM ...

Abbacia
Scm̄ ...

Betania
Iericho

Gazre

Bethleē

Terra egipti

Gsepulchr Abrahe
Ebron

Introitus egipti

Solda

babilonie
persay
Soldani ... damasci

Figure 51. Pietro Vesconte's map of
Palestine with grid. MS. Tanner 190,
fols. 205v–206r (Italian, 1321).

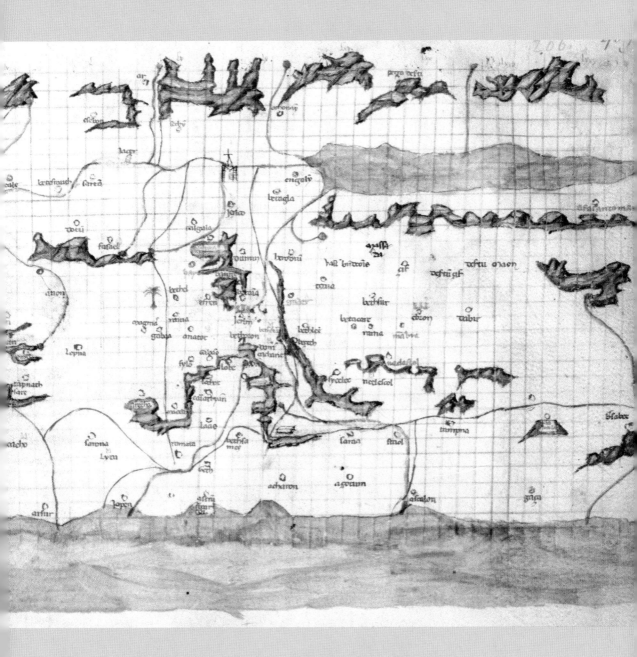

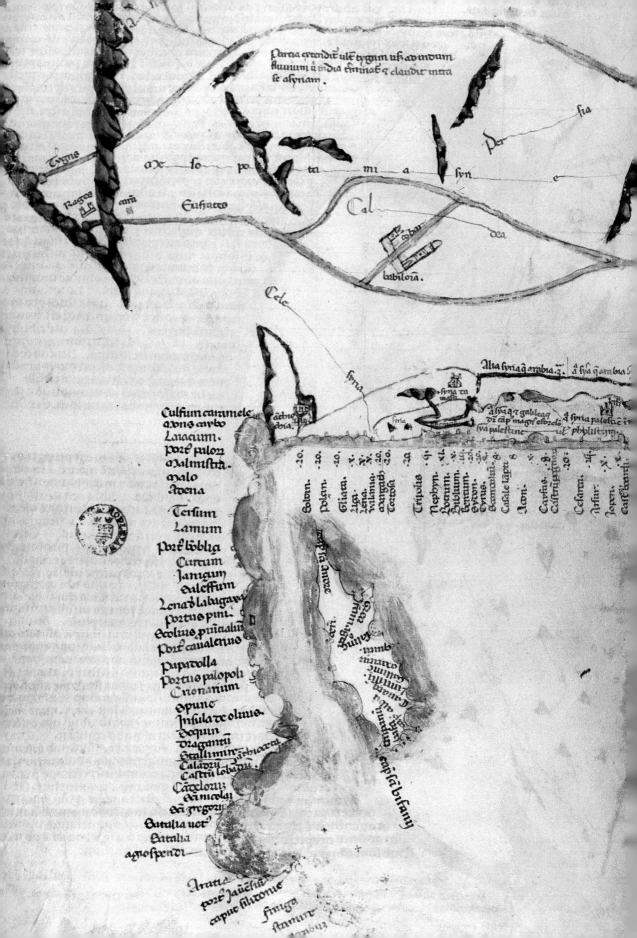

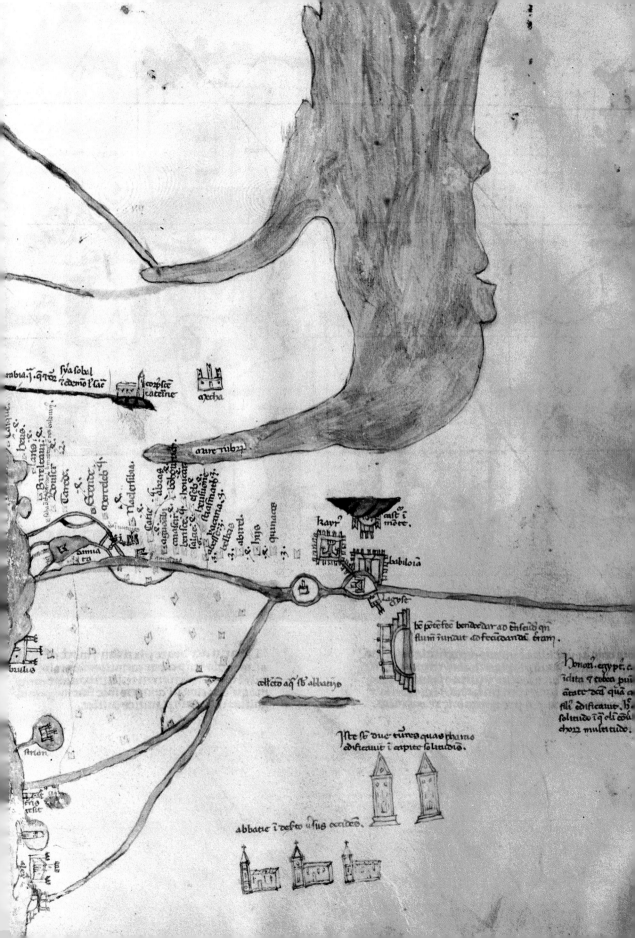

rabia: j. qnoz sya sobal
7 edno l'ac
comple̅t̅e
catt̅ine
axcha

are rubz̅

la Birelan̅s:
louer
Tanea
Stance
axeld c̅

Tadeisibas
Sane dibag bolomoz
exaghnodiz bouhant
enifer honoua̅
salae efez
bulione
klasmach 7
abocana .3.
telbes .3.
abtel .3.
hya
quinaca .3.

kayr?
cast i
moce

babiloia

amilta

lagybe

be poe̅st̅e bendedar ad dnseud qn
flum iundat co feacdandu̅ bram

stion

colleco aq̅ 7 b̅ abbatin̅o

Honor̅ egypt̅ c̅
idita 7 tena pri
a̅tate dci qua̅
fili edificauit h̅
solitudo tq oli edu
choi̅ multitudo

bnulio

Jste so oue cures quas phaus
edificauit i capite soliudis.

abbatie i reb̅o ulus cende̅s.

eno̅
resi̅

Figure 52 *previous page*. Pietro Vesconte's map of the eastern Mediterranean. East is at the top. the island of Cyprus at the lower left, and the Nile River and Red Sea are shown at the right. MS. Tanner 190, fol. 204v–205r (Italian, 1321).

Figure 53 *right*. Pietro Vesconte's city plan of Jerusalem. MS. Tanner 190, fol. 206v (Italian, 1321).

wooden covers inlaid with ivory and ebony geometric designs. The atlas is protected by a black leather case ornately decorated with tooled designs and lettering (see Figure 56). The seven sea charts depict the Black Sea, the Mediterranean, the Atlantic coasts of north Africa and Europe, and England and Ireland, and all of them are bound with south at the top. The atlas begins with paintings of an angel and the Virgin Mary, and concludes with paintings of Saint Mark and Saint Paul – the only figures in the entire atlas as no animal or human forms are depicted on the charts themselves.

We know little about the origin of these maps or the techniques by which they were constructed. The list of ports, however, whose names are written around the coastlines, are to be found in sets of sailing directions called portolans, which pre-date the surviving charts. The compass, which was in common use in Europe by the year 1200, probably played a role in the construction of the portolans and the charts. A characteristic feature of the latter is the compass rose, an often decorative roundel from which radiate a set of rhumb lines or compass-bearings, based on the eight main winds and their subordinate winds. Navigational instructions exist, telling pilots how to adjust their course by the compass when diverted by bad weather or other nautical mischance. The earliest charts were spare and undecorated, reflecting their utilitarian character, but they soon acquired pictorial features, and some, especially those of the Catalan school, are awe-inspiring works of art.

The Turkish counterparts of the sea charts are the lovely navigational maps of the Mediterranean in the *Kitāb-i Baḥriyye* ('Book of Maritime Matters') by Pīrī Re'īs (d. 1554), an atlas of charts for small segments of the Mediterranean, accompanied by sailing instructions covering the entire sea (Figure 57). Pīrī Re'īs prepared two versions of the work, the second having the latest information then available regarding the discovery of America.

We do not know the author of a mid-fourteenth century map of Britain, usually called the Gough Map after one of its owners (Figure 58). The map includes a great number of rivers and some 600 towns and villages. The towns are linked by a network of lines which appear to be roads, though some important roads are missing and others are problematic. On each section of road is recorded the distance in local miles, which varied in length, and there is no attempt to adjust the map to represent the scale. The southern and eastern coasts are well

Figure 56. Black leather case, with tooled design and lettering, for holding a set of seven 15th-century Spanish sea charts. MS. Douce 390, case.

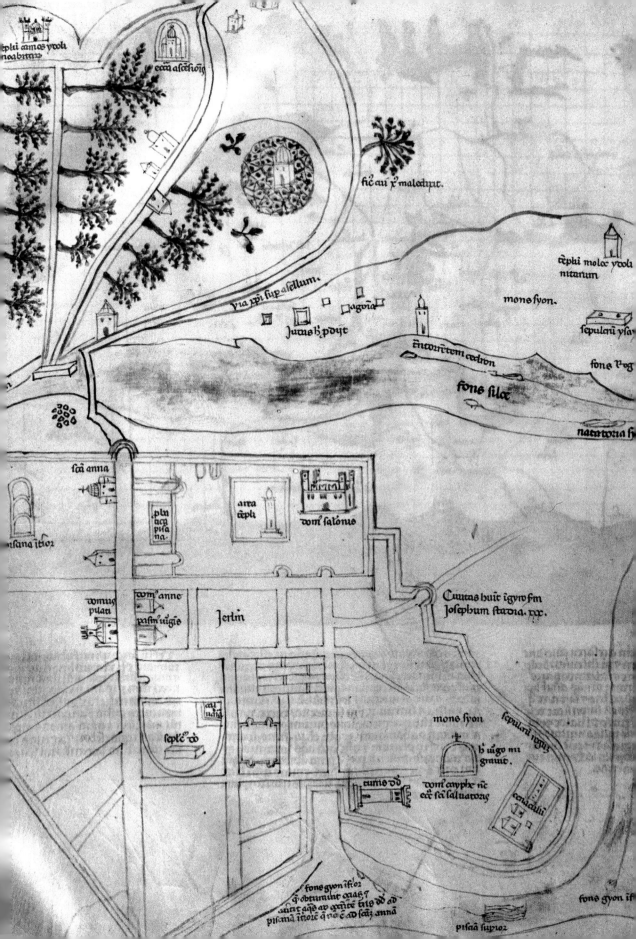

tepli amos yroli noabitant

ecta ascensiois

hic an͛ x͛ maledixit.

tepli moloc yroli nitarium

mons syon.

via xpi sup asellum.

Iuras h͛ pdyt

agoia

sepulcrū ysa

intouitem cedron

fons Reg

fons silce

natatoria h͛

scā anna

pisana itior

pla aca pisana

area tepli

dom salonis

domus pilati

dom͛ anne pasin͛uigis

Ierlm

Ciuitas huic igitur sm Iosephum stadia. xx.

caudig

septem do

mons syon

sepulcrū regis

b͛ uirgo migrauit.

cumis do

dom͛ cayphe nc ecc scē saluatone

cenaculii

fons gyon ist or h͛ obturunt onax͛ 7 uaint aqd ap gttere tris do od pisma itioit q n͛ c͛ ad scāz annā

fons gyon is

pisā supior

Figure 54 *right*. A sea chart showing Corsica, Sardinia, Italy, Sicily, and North Africa, from a Spanish 15th-century case of 7 charts. MS. Douce 390, chart no. 5.

Figure 55 *below right*. Italian sea chart of the entire Mediterranean drawn by Placido Caloiro about 1665. Palm trees decorate North Africa. On the neck of the chart there is a medallion with Mother and Child. The Holy Land is designated by three crosses, while the island of Rhodes (near the south-west coast of Turkey) is marked by a cross, more than a century after the Knights Hospitalers ceased to occupy it in 1523. MS. Canon. Ital. 140, pp. 3–4.

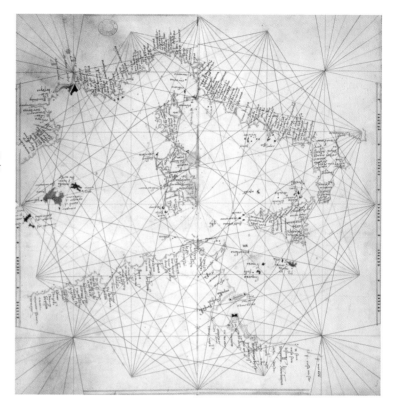

drawn and may have been based on a sea chart. The factual nature of
this map and its lack of any superfluous ornament suggest that it was
intended for practical use. There may have been other copies as well,
as we find it used as a source in the making of some later maps of
Britain. These examples of medieval regional maps demonstrate a
practical side to mapping, not always evident when looking at world
maps.

The sixteenth century saw a great increase in the production of
regional maps, some of which were made to accompany editions of
Ptolemy's *Geography*. These so-called 'tabulae modernae' were updated
versions, mostly with the addition of modern place-names, to
Ptolemy's own regional maps, whose toponymy was naturally outdated. The earliest tabulae modernae were of northern Europe, an area
poorly known to the Romans, and of more familiar lands like France,
Spain, and Italy.

Figure 57 *above*. Thessaloniki (left)
and Mount Athos (right) from the
Book of Maritime Matters by Pīrī Re'īs
(d. 1554). MS. d'Orville 543, fols. 7b–
8a (1587 [996H]).

Figure 58. The 'Gough' map of
Britain, showing 600 towns and villages
connected by a network of roads.
MS. Gough Gen. Top.16 (English, 14th
century).

12

Travellers and Traders

Although long-distance travel during the Middle Ages was hazardous and slow, people continued to set forth on journeys of various lengths. One motive for travel was pilgrimage. While a trip to the nearest shrine was always meritorious, the ultimate pilgrimage was to visit the holiest of all Christian sites in Jerusalem. As early as the fourth century we have reports of pilgrimages and an itinerary, originating in Bordeaux, suggests the best route to follow. In the seventh century the bishop Adomnan wrote a book on the holy places, based on the first-person experience of another bishop, Arculf, a few years earlier. Adomnan's account was illustrated with 'measured drawings,' of the churches of the Ascension and the Holy Sepulchre. These drawings were incorporated into a similar work by Bede, *De locis sanctis,* in the next century. Muslims were inspired to travel by their obligation to make a pilgrimage to Mecca. As Islam spread beyond the original Arabian homeland, this journey became a more difficult proposition, but Muslim pilgrims regularly came to Mecca from all parts of Africa, Spain, Persia, and India.

Another motive for travel was commerce. 'There are only seven "climes" in the whole extent of the world,' wrote the English monk and chronicler, Matthew Paris, in 1241, 'namely those of the Indians, Ethiopians or Moors, Egyptians, Jerusalemites, Greeks, Romans, and French, and there are none so remotely situated in the whole of the habitable part of the world, that merchants will not find their way among them'.[14] Riding on donkeys, trudging under the weight of a backpack, setting sail in dubious-looking boats, merchants continued to make their way about the world, buying here and selling there. Trading galleys from the Italian cities plied the Mediterranean, while Catalan traders regularly crossed the Atlas Mountains into the oasis towns of the Sahara, looking for gold. In the French territory of

Champagne in the twelfth and thirteenth centuries fairs were held six times a year at regularly scheduled intervals, attracting merchants from all over Europe. The goods came from even farther afield, including Chinese silks, Indian spices, Sri Lankan rubies, and African ivory. In Cairo a storehouse of documents has been found, revealing a network of Jewish traders operating in Spain, North Africa, the Levant, and India in the eleventh and twelfth centuries. To the north the sea-going Norsemen were looking for plunder more than trade. Their incredible journeys through the northern seas reached to Iceland, Greenland, and America, all done apparently without the aid of maps.

Muslims and Christians rubbed shoulders, not always amicably, in the divided kingdom of Spain and in the multicultural island of Sicily. The Crusades, launched at the end of the eleventh century, brought many Europeans into intimate contact with the Islamic society of the eastern Mediterranean. Although the original motivation was religious warfare, the Crusades brought in their wake traders, settlers, even scholars. Works such as Jacques de Vitry's (c.1160–1240) history of the crusades included material on the geography of the Middle East, and the customs and religion of the people. The besieged Christians in the Holy Land sought help from further east, and embassies were sent to the sons of Genghis Khan in Central Asia. No alliance was ever cemented, but important information about the large eastern continent filtered back to Europe, filling its vast spaces with real towns, mountain ranges, and rivers. Hopeful missionaries were dispatched in an attempt to convert the Tartars to Christianity, and for a while the Church maintained bishops and monasteries in several cities of the east.

Two of the most ambitious medieval travellers were Marco Polo, a Venetian, and Ibn Baṭṭūtah, a Moroccan. Both covered thousands of miles and saw a large part of the known world. Their books circulated widely within their own cultures and to some extent beyond. Marco Polo went with his father and uncle on their second expedition to Cathay (see Figure 59). Leaving home in 1270, he spent a quarter of a century in Asia, travelling from Mongolia into China and eventually sailing back across the Indian Ocean from the East through the Persian Gulf and then overland to the Mediterranean. His journeys were facilitated by the widespread empire of the Great Khan, which en-forced a kind of rough peace in Central Asia. A golden tablet provided by the Khan enabled the traveller to obtain horses, provisions, and an armed escort. Marco's work, *Le Divisament dou Monde* ('Description of the World'), was packed with information about the kingdom of

Figure 59. The Polos leave Venice, from *Li Livres du Graunt Caam* (Marco Polo's *Travels*) by artist Johannes and his school. MS. Bodl. 264, fol. 218r (English, c. 1400).

Cathay, a world of high civilization and great riches largely unknown to the West. His description of the desirable products of the East and the low prices for which they could be obtained put stars into the eyes of Western merchants willing to brave desert sandstorms and snow-covered mountain-ranges in quest of profits. In contrast to Marco, Ibn Baṭṭūṭah (1304–68) began his travels in the spirit of piety as a pilgrim to Mecca, but he continued to wander for almost thirty years, driven by a desire to see and learn about new places. Before returning home, he visited most of the countries of the Islamic world from southern Africa to eastern Asia. The universal use of Arabic and the traveller's status as a judge trained in the law gave him a passport to royal courts wherever he went. As Ibn Baṭṭūṭah was on his way home through Syria in 1348, he was the horrified witness of the ravages of the Black Death. By the time he got to Cairo he found that bustling city eerily deserted, having lost almost half its people to the plague.

The devastation of the plague and the break-up of the Mongol empire into warring factions brought a temporary end to long-distance travel. For a while people had to make do with travel fantasies, such as the tales of Sir John Mandeville, whose purported travels surpassed even those of Marco and Ibn Baṭṭūṭah. Sir John was unworthy to enter the earthly Paradise, he tells us, but he did get close enough to hear the waters of the Four Rivers falling from its height. Whereas Marco and Ibn Baṭṭūṭah had not been successful in seeing the monstrous races that were part of medieval lore, Mandeville showed no such restraint and gleefully described to his awe-struck readers the enormities of the human race, both physical and sociological. The illustrators of his work, which was finished in the mid-fourteenth century, took full advantage of this aspect of it. The book was immensely popular, surviving in over 300 manuscripts.

Travellers generally did not make use of maps in the Middle Ages, but sought the advice of local guides or joined groups going in the same direction, such as the pilgrims in *The Canterbury Tales*. Instead, medieval maps were used by scholars, such as those wishing to interpret the Bible or to understand works of history. Even the marine charts seem to have been used originally by businessmen and administrators at home, and only occasionally taken to sea. Travellers had, however, an impact on how maps were made. By the end of the fourteenth century Marco Polo's description of Asia was showing up on most world maps, transforming the classically derived picture of that continent. Travellers also challenged certain assumptions about the world, such as the idea of

Ci commence li liures du grant Caam qui parole de la grandit Ermenie de perse
et des tartars et dynde. Et des grans merueilles qui par le monde sont.

Pour sauoir la pure verite des
diuerses regions du monde, si
prenez cest liure si trouuerez les
grandisnmes merueilles qui sont
escriptes en la grant hermenie
et de perse, et destartas, + dynde
et de mruites autres prouinces, si comme noz liures
uous contera tout par ordre des que mes sires marc pol
es et nobles si toies de ueue raconte pource que il
uit, mais auques il y a choses.

Qu'il ne uit pas, mais il entendi d'ommes certains par uerite. Et pour ce
metrons nous les choses ueues pour
ueues. Et l'entendu pour entendue
a ce que nr liure soit urais et uerrai

bles sauz nule mencouge. Et chascuis qui ce liure ora
ou lira le doit croire, pource que toutes sont choses ue-
ritables. Car ie uous fais a sauoir que puis que nre
sire diex fist adam le premier pre ne fu oncques de
nul homme generacion qui tant seust ne cerchast
des diuerses parties du monde come cestui me sire marc
pol en soe et pource pensa que ce seroit grans maus se
ce ne fist metre en escint ce que il auoit ueu et oi par la
rite. A ce que lautre gent que ne sont ueue oi le sa-
chent par cest liure. Et si uous di quil le uoura a ce
sauoir, en ces duises parties bien. xxvi. ans le quel
liure puis que demoura suz en la carcer de geneua
retraire par ordre par me sire rasta pila. Qui en cele
meismes prison estoit au temps que il couroit de
crist. ap̃l. CC. + iiij. et xxix. ans a l'incarnacion

uninhabitable north and south polar zones, and the unendurable heat of the torrid belt. In the fifteenth century the Portuguese launched a determined effort to explore the coast of Africa, changing its image completely by delineating its coastline and discovering that it could be circumnavigated. Features of medieval maps, such as the inaccessible garden of Paradise and the mysterious hydrology of the Four Rivers flowing from it, were increasingly difficult to maintain against the experience of travellers. Finally, at the end of the fifteenth century, the three-continent world of time immemorial suddenly became a five-continent world, and the T-O map was gone forever. Although people had long understood that the world was a sphere and that there might be land on the other side, the actual experience of sailing around it and finding whole lands full of previously unknown nations was a transforming and unsettling discovery.

Conclusion

The medieval worlds of Islam and Christianity had inherited from Greek civilization a common fund of scientific knowledge, which described the heavens and the earth in both theoretical and practical terms. The Greek inheritance came to the Latin West first via Roman popularizers and encyclopaedists, and early Christian neo-Platonists. The Islamic world received its Greek legacy via Byzantium, as well as the civilisations of India and Persia. By the ninth century, Arabs had at their disposal a complete library of Greek scientific writings, including those of Ptolemy and Aristotle. In the twelfth century contact between the two societies, mostly in Spain, brought increased intellectual riches to the West, where the newly translated works (and accompanying original Arabic discourses) were received with great excitement. The results, however, of these two periods of translation and absorption of classical ideas were quite distinct, with each society retaining its own cultural, religious, and intellectual slant.

The Ptolemaic system of astronomy reigned in both East and West. As early as the ninth century the *Almagest* was the subject of intense study among the scholars of Baghdad, who incorporated it into their world view and did sophisticated work in both mathematics and astronomy. A surprising exception was Ptolemy's ingenious design for a celestial globe that would not become outdated with the precession of the equinoxes. This idea was overlooked by all subsequent Arabic readers and commentators on the *Almagest*. The desire to make improved astrological predictions led to increasingly precise observations of the movements of the heavenly bodies. In the West this did not begin until the reception of the *Almagest* in the twelfth century. The gradual accumulation of data made it clear that even Ptolemy's epicycles were not sufficient to account for all the vagaries of celestial motion, and thus the system was eventually undermined.

Despite the availability of Ptolemy's *Geography* in the Islamic world, his work was apparently not fully understood, as it was not employed in map-making. Medieval Islamic maps were abstract constructions with little devotion to representing geographical forms or precise distances. Ptolemy's elaborate tables of coordinates, while used for casting horoscopes and for determination of Qibla, were not used to construct maps, which were more loosely organized according to the seven astronomically-defined 'climes'. Geographical forms were for the most part geometrical and abstract, such as the 'Balkhī school' products or the oval Mediterranean of a century later, or the maps were really graphic itineraries, such as the earliest 'maps' of Sicily and Cyprus.

Maps in early medieval Christendom, particularly world maps, were attempts to explore theological and historical aspects of space, rather than to make scale-models of the physical world. In the great *mappae mundi* of the thirteenth century, the world was drawn in the embrace of Christ or being presided over by him, and many of the places shown were of religious significance. Thus the cities of Sodom and Gomorrah, long sunk beneath the Dead Sea in punishment for their crimes, still appear on medieval maps, as do the city of Troy and the Tower of Babel. Paradise, usually placed in the privileged position at the eastern summit of the map, shows Adam and Eve in the act of original sin, the deed which led the human race to be expelled from Eden and to the beginning of time and the occupation of geographical space. Their presence shows a kind of 'stopped-time' aspect of medieval *mappae mundi*, where the past was ever present. The inclusion of Old Testament sites (such as Mount Sinai where Moses received the Law), places connected with the life and death of Christ, and the locations where the apostles preached showed the sequence of Christian religious time, culminating in the Last Days. On many maps the birthplace of the dreaded Antichrist is shown, along with his allies Gog and Magog, while the Hereford Cathedral map has Christ in Judgement enthroned at the top of the map.

In contrast, Islamic maps were completely devoid of theological content, being directed more to the mundane purposes of trade and empire or as guides for arm-chair travellers. While Islamic writers speculated on Paradise and the Four Rivers, these features did not appear on their maps. Islamic maps were not ornamented with the pictures which adorned so many European maps, nor did they represent events in the history of Islam. They seem to have been designed strictly for utilitarian rather than philosophical purposes.

It was not until the thirteenth century that Europeans began to draw maps based on the faithful rendering of travelled space. These are the marine charts, the oldest survivor of which dates from 1275. Because of the sudden appearance of these charts and their early perfection, it was speculated that they were of Arabic origin, but no similar work of cartography has been found in the Arabic body of maps of the same period. Possibly Arab travellers and traders supplied information for the marine charts, but there is no evidence that they had any impact on their form. The compass, which seemed to provide much of the data for the making of the sea charts, is of unknown origin. Long thought to be an Islamic borrowing from the Far East, its precise line of transmission is obscure. Then, in the fifteenth century, when Ptolemy's work was revived in the West, Ptolemaic geography was communicated again to the Islamic East almost as a new work. From this point on, Islamic, particularly Turkish, maps and European ones evolved side by side, mutually influencing and enhancing one another.

The Copernican revolution of the sixteenth century transformed man's conception of the universe and his position within it. Not only was the earth displaced from the centre of the universe and demoted to a middle-sized planet revolving around a rather ordinary star, but the laws of terrestrial physics were now understood to operate in the celestial sphere as well. This philosophical shift, and its subsequent development by Galileo, Johannes Kepler, and Isaac Newton, did not play a significant role in scientific thinking in the Islamic world until the end of the eighteenth century, though the heliocentric theory was occasionally mentioned alongside the Ptolemaic earth-centred one. In Europe, on the other hand, from the end of the seventeenth century, a mechanistic philosophy of nature and a scientific method based on observation and experiment dominated much of the learned discourse. The medieval view of the cosmos—crystal spheres, heavenly harmonies, and lowly earth—was doomed.

Notes

1   C.S. Lewis, *The Discarded Image: An Introduction to Medieval and Renaissance Literature* (Cambridge, 1964), pp. 98–99.

2   Dante, *Paradiso*, XXII and XXVIII, trans. John Ciardi (New York, 1961), pp. 250 and 308.

3   *Troilus and Cressida*, Act I, scene 3.

4   *The Odyssey,* Book V, trans. E. V. Rieu (Baltimore, 1946), p. 95.

5   Quotation is from the anonymous *Kitāb Gharā'ib al-funūn wa-mulaḥ al-'uyūn* (*Book of Curiosities*), compiled about 1020–1050, in Oxford, Bodleian Library, MS. Arab 90, fol. 14a (twelfth–thirteenth century).

6   This passage from Ibn Khallikān is discussed in detail by David A. King, 'Origin of the Astrolabe according to the Medieval Islamic Sources', *Journal for the History of Arabic Science* 5 (1981), 48–83 (esp. 60-61).

7   For Aristotle's views on this topic, see *De caelo* II.i.

8   al-Bīrunī, *The Chronology of Ancient Nations*, trans. Edward Sachau (London, 1879), p. 116 (translation slightly emended).

9   The quotation is from the *Histories*, Book V, chs. 49-50, trans. Aubrey de Selincourt (Baltimore, 1954).

10 Pliny, *Natural History*, III.16.

11 For the relevant passage in the *City of God*, see Book XVI.9.

12 The quotation is from the anonymous *Kitāb al-Jughrāfiyah* in Rabat, al-Khizanah al-Āmmah, MS. 770, fol. 5b. Translation is that of Gabriel Ferrand, slightly emended; see *Encyclopaedia of Islam*, 1st edn., ed. M. Th. Houtsma (Leiden, 1938), vol. 4, p. 1107.

13 For the reference to Bede, see *De Natura Rerum*, ch. 46. See Washington Irving, *The Life and Voyages of Christopher Columbus*, ed. John Harmon McElroy (Boston, 1981), pp. 47-53, for the relevant scene. For Irving's role in promoting the idea that medieval people were Flat-Earthers, see Jeffrey Burton Russell, *Inventing the Flat Earth: Columbus and Modern Historians* (New York, 1991), pp. 51–7.

14 Matthew Paris, *Chronica Majora,* in *Matthew Paris's English History,* trans. J. A. Giles (London, 1852-54), vol. 1, p. 348

Further Reading

Edson, Evelyn, *Mapping Time and Space: How Medieval Mapmakers viewed their World*, British Library Studies in Map History 1 (London, 1997).

Evans, James, *The History and Practice of Ancient Astronomy* (New York, 1998).

Harley, J.B. and David Woodward, *Cartography in Prehistoric, Ancient, and Medieval Europe and the Mediterranean*, History of Cartography 1 (Chicago, 1987).

Harley, J.B. and David Woodward, *Cartography in Traditional Islamic and South Asian Societies*, History of Cartography, 2.1 (Chicago, 1992).

Harvey, P.D.A., *Medieval Maps* (London, 1991).

Heinen, Anton M., *Islamic Cosmology* (Beirut, 1982).

Johns, Jeremy, and Emilie Savage-Smith, 'The *Book of Curiosities*: A Newly Discovered Series of Islamic Maps', *Imago Mundi* 55 (2003), 7–24. See also <http://www.bodley.ox.ac.uk/bookofcuriosities>.

King, David A., *Islamic Astronomical Instruments*, Variorum CS 253 (London, 1987).

King, David A., *World-Maps for Finding the Direction and Distance to Mecca: Innovation and Tradition in Islamic Science* (Leiden, 1999).

Larner, John, *Marco Polo and the Discovery of the World* (New Haven, 1999).

Lindbergh, David C., *The Beginnings of Western Science: The European Scientific Tradition in Philosophical, Religious, and Institutional Context, 600 BC to AD 1450* (Chicago, 1992).

Maddison, Francis, and Emilie Savage-Smith, *Science, Tools & Magic*, Nasser D. Khalili Collection of Islamic Art 12, (London and Oxford, 1997).

Murdoch, John E., *Album of Science: Antiquity and the Middle Ages* (New York, 1984).

Nasr, Seyyed Hossein, *An Introduction to Islamic Cosmological Doctrines* (Cambridge, MA, 1964).

Ptolemy, Claudius, *Almagest,* trans. and ed. G. J. Toomer (New York and Berlin, 1984).

Ptolemy, Claudius, *Ptolemy's Geography: An Annotated History of the Theoretical Chapters*, trans. and ed. J. Lennert Berggren and Alexander Jones (Princeton, 2000).

Ptolemy, Claudius, *The Geography,* trans. and ed. E. L. Stevenson (New York, 1932, rpt. 1991).

Romm, James S., *The Edges of the Earth in Ancient Thought* (Princeton, 1992).

Savage-Smith, Emilie, 'Memory and Maps', in *Culture and Memory in Early and Medieval Islam: A Festschrift in honour of Wilferd Madelung,* ed. F. Daftary and J. Meri (London, 2003), pp. 109–27.

Savage-Smith, Emilie, *Islamicate Celestial Globes: Their History, Construction, and Use,* Smithsonian Studies in History and Technology 46 (Washington, D.C., 1985).

Southern, Richard W., *Robert Grosseteste: The Growth of an English Mind in Medieval Europe* (Oxford, 1986).

Tibbetts, G.R., *Arab Navigation in the Indian Ocean before the Coming of the Portuguese* (London, 1971).

Turner, Anthony J., *Mathematical Instruments in Antiquity and the Middle Ages* (London, 1994).

Vlastos, Gregory, *Plato's Universe* (Seattle, 1975).

Westrem, Scott D., *The Hereford Map: A transcription and translation of the legends with commentary* (Turnhout, 2001).

emilie.savage-smith@orinst.ox.ac.uk
Research interests: Islamic
https://www.~~oint~~ orinst.ox.ac.uk/people/emilie-savage-smith

St. Cross College
Oxford
61 St. Giles
Oxford OX1 3LZ

Postal Address
St. Cross College
61 St. Giles
Oxford
44(0) 1865 278490

Dean Dr. Heather Hamill
heather.hamill@sociology.ox.ac.uk

The Oriental Institute   University of Oxford
Pusey Lane   St. Cross College
Oxford. OX1 2LE